ANNE WILLAN'S
LOOK&COOK

Fish Classics

ANNE WILLAN'S
LOOK&COOK

Fish Classics

DORLING KINDERSLEY
LONDON • NEW YORK • STUTTGART

A DORLING KINDERSLEY BOOK

Created and Produced by
CARROLL & BROWN LIMITED
5 Lonsdale Road
London NW6 6RA

Editorial Director Jeni Wright
Editors Norma MacMillan
Sally Poole
Stella Vayne
Art Editor Vicky Zentner
Designers Lucy De Rosa
Mary Staples
Alan Watt
Lisa Webb
Production Editor Wendy Rogers

First American Edition, 1993
10 9 8 7 6 5 4 3 2 1

Published in the United States by
Dorling Kindersley, Inc., 232 Madison Avenue
New York, New York 10016

Willan, Anne.
    Fish classics / by Anne Willan. – 1st American ed.
        p.   cm. – Anne Willan's Look & cook
    Includes index.
    ISBN 1-56458-190-X
        1. Cookery (Fish)   I. Title.   II. Series: Willan, Anne.
Look and cook.
TX747.W554   1993
641.6'92 – dc20   92-53453
                                                                                      CIP

Reproduced by Colourscan, Singapore
Printed and bound in Italy by A. Mondadori, Verona

CONTENTS

FISH

THE LOOK & COOK APPROACH

Welcome to **Fish Classics** and the *Look & Cook* series. These volumes are designed to be the simplest, most informative cookbooks you'll ever own. They are the closest I can come to sharing my techniques for cooking my own favorite recipes without actually being with you in the kitchen looking over your shoulder.

Equipment and ingredients often determine whether or not you can cook a particular dish, so *Look & Cook* illustrates everything you need at the beginning of each recipe. You'll see at a glance how long a recipe takes to cook, how many servings it makes, what the finished dish looks like, and how much preparation can be done ahead. When you start to cook, you'll find the preparation and cooking are organized into easy-to-follow steps. Each stage is color-coded and everything is shown in photographs with brief text to go with each step. You will never be in doubt about what it is you are doing, why you are doing it, or how it should look.

EQUIPMENT

INGREDIENTS

🍽 SERVES 4-6   🍲 WORK TIME 25-35 MINUTES   ☕ COOKING TIME 20-30 MINUTES

I've also included helpful hints and ideas under "Anne Says". These may list an alternative ingredient or piece of equipment, or sometimes the reason for using a certain method is explained, or there is some advice on mastering a particular technique. Similarly, if there is a crucial stage in a recipe when things can go wrong, I've included some warnings called "Take Care".

Many of the photographs are annotated to pinpoint why certain pieces of equipment work best, or how the food should look at that stage of cooking. Because presentation is so important, a picture of the finished dish and serving suggestions are at the end of each recipe.

Thanks to all this information, you can't go wrong. I'll be with you every step of the way. So please come with me into the kitchen to look, cook, and create some delicious **Fish Classics**.

Anne Willan

WHY FISH?

Fish continues to grow in popularity for a number of reasons: nutritionally, it meets today's health criteria; the quality of fresh fish on the market is constantly improving; and through better handling techniques and rapid distribution from the oceans, lakes, and rivers the available choice is increasing. Fish seems to be a culinary challenge, but the simplicity of the recipes in this book will surprise you, showing fish is easy to prepare and offers endless variety, with an enticing range of flavors and textures.

RECIPE CHOICE

These recipes represent an array of easy fish dishes, featuring classic favorites and contemporary flavors. All the recipes are ideal for today's busy lifestyle, offering a delectable selection of quick, healthy, and inventive dishes that put the pleasure back into cooking fish. You will find that they are all appropriate to serve as main courses, while some could also be offered as substantial first courses. Below is a summary of the recipes you will find in this volume, which includes recipes based on fish fillets and pieces of fish, as well as whole fish.

FISH FILLETS AND PIECES

Broiled Tuna Steaks with Salsa: tuna steaks are marinated, then broiled to serve with a colorful salsa of tomatoes, corn, red bell pepper, coriander, and onion. *Broiled Swordfish with Fennel and Sun-Dried Tomatoes*: sun-dried tomatoes and fennel, cooked to melting tenderness, complement broiled swordfish steaks. *Crisp-Sided Salmon with Fresh Coriander Pesto*: salmon is fried on one side only for a contrast of crunchy skin with a lightly cooked top. The salmon is served with an emerald-green pesto sauce made with fresh coriander. *Crisp-Sided Salmon with Garlic Sabayon*: salmon fillets fried on one side are broiled with a fluffy sabayon sauce flavored with garlic, white wine, and sweet vermouth. *Spicy Fish Stew*: pieces of monkfish and a selection of vegetables mix with apple, shredded coconut, and plenty of spices for an exotic casserole. *Spicy Fish Stew with Potatoes*: peas and peanuts add crunch to this hearty grouper stew, with potatoes for body. *Spicy Fish Stew with Bell Peppers*: three colors of bell pepper highlight this grouper stew.

Oriental Halibut in a Paper Case: black beans and Chinese flavorings garnish white fish fillets, baked on a bed of crisp snow peas, all enclosed in an attractive parchment paper package. *Thai-Style Halibut in a Paper Case*: Thai flavorings combine with this French cooking technique for an unusual and flavorful dish. *Tuna and Bacon Kebabs*: cubes of tuna are marinated, wrapped in bacon, threaded on skewers with cherry tomatoes, then broiled to serve on a background salad of fresh spinach and sliced mango. *Monkfish and Bacon Kebabs*: cubes of monkfish combine with bacon and wedges of red onion for these kebabs. *New England Cod and Mussel Chowder*: mussels in their shells and diced bacon add color and flavor to this rich and creamy white fish stew. *Manhattan Cod and Mussel Chowder*: a lively fish stew made with tomatoes, garlic, white wine, and thyme. *Perfect Fish and Chips*: the British favorite of cod fillets deep-fried in a light beer batter, served with crisp thick-cut French fries. *Tempura-Style Fish with Sweet Potatoes*: Japanese-style coating for fish, with crisply fried sweet potato slices on the side and an oriental dipping sauce. *English Fish Pie*: an English inspiration made from flaked white fish, shrimp, and hard-boiled eggs in a white sauce, topped with mashed potato, and baked in the oven until golden brown. *Individual Fish Crumbles*: a homey topping of rolled oats with parsley and Parmesan cheese makes a crunchy contrast to a filling of chunks of fish and shrimp in white sauce baked in individual casserole dishes. *Saltimbocca of Salmon*: this delicious variation of traditional veal saltimbocca uses marinated salmon slices rolled around smoked salmon and basil leaves, then sautéed in butter to serve with a tomato-basil garnish. *Paupiettes of Sole*: lemon sole fillets rolled with smoked salmon and steamed. *Roast Monkfish with Garlic and Chili Sauces*: plump fillets of monkfish are marinated in olive oil mixed with fresh oregano and thyme, then roasted and sliced to serve with garlic and spicy chili sauces. *Broiled Monkfish Scaloppine with Garlic and Chili Sauces*: the same pungent sauces complement thinly sliced fillets of monkfish, which are quickly cooked under a hot broiler. *Seafood Lasagne*: a delicious version of lasagne made with layers of sole, shrimp, scallops, and noodles, baked in a creamy sauce flavored with mushrooms, tomatoes, shallots, and white wine and topped with cheese. *Smoked Trout and Spinach Lasagne*: pieces of smoked trout flavor this version of seafood lasagne, made colorful with green spinach pasta. *Steamed Braided Fish with Warm Vinaigrette*: three varieties of fish are cut into strips, shaped into a delicate braid, and steamed to serve with a warm vinaigrette. *Panaché of Steamed Fish with Warm Sherry Vinaigrette*: a trio of fish with different colored skins are steamed for this "panaché", or selection. *Monkfish Américaine*: monkfish, sometimes called "the poor man's lobster", is served in the classic sauce of tomato, garlic, and Cognac. *Salt Cod Américaine*: Américaine sauce highlights chunks of salt cod served with rice pilaf. *Turbans of Sole with Wild Mushroom Mousse*: sole fillets are wrapped turban-style around a delectable wild mushroom mousse, baked in white wine, and served with a fresh coriander butter sauce. *Turbans of Flounder with Spinach Mousse*: bright green spinach mousse is the filling for white flounder fillets, with a simple tomato butter sauce as accompaniment. *Two-Color Fish Terrine with Citrus-Ginger Sauce*: a delicate pink salmon mousseline, wrapped with white bands of sole fillet, hides a mosaic of smoked salmon and sole, and is perfectly complemented by a tangy citrus sauce. *Individual Fish Terrines*: ramekins lined with thinly sliced fresh salmon are filled with a smooth mousseline made with white fish.

WHOLE FISH

Bouillabaisse: the world-famous Mediterranean stew includes an international variety of fish, accented by saffron, garlic, fennel, orange, and Pernod. *Creole Bouillabaisse*: oysters and crayfish join the fish in this version of bouillabaisse from Louisiana. *Sautéed Trout with Hazelnuts*: crunchy browned hazelnuts top whole trout sautéed in butter in this rapid recipe. *Sautéed Trout with Capers, Lemon, and Croûtons*: piquant capers, lemon, and golden brown croûtons add flavor to pan-fried trout. *Poached Salmon with Watercress Sauce*: fresh salmon is poached and served whole for a dramatic presentation, with a refreshing watercress sauce on the side. *Pan-Fried Mackerel Coated in Rolled Oats*: a traditional Scottish recipe using whole mackerel cut into fillets, covered in rolled oats, and fried for a crispy coating. *Almond-Coated Perch*: succulent perch fillets are coated with slivered almonds and pan-fried. *Broiled Trout with Orange and Mustard Glaze*: small whole fish, onions, and mushrooms are brushed with a tangy glaze of orange and mustard, then broiled. *Broiled Cod Steaks with Maître d'Hôtel Butter*: butter flavored with parsley, shallots, and lemon juice complements broiled fish steaks. *Sole Bonne Femme*: this most delicious of fish dishes is made from sole fillets poached in fish stock enriched with white wine and served with a rich mushroom and cream sauce. *Fillets of Sole with Mushrooms and Tomatoes*: mushrooms and tomatoes are added to a creamy velouté sauce topping sole fillets.

EQUIPMENT

There are many different types of fish, but you will not need many items of specialized equipment for these recipes. Most important is a fish filleting knife with a thin flexible blade, used to fillet fish, and to trim and cut it into pieces or thin slices. A chef's knife is also necessary for cutting and trimming fish and cutting up fish bones for stock. Be sure to sharpen all your knives on a steel each time you use them. Metal tongs and a wide metal spatula, preferably with slots for draining, will help you turn fish fillets or transfer them from the pan.

Your baking dishes will come into use as various sizes are needed for the assortment of recipes cooked in the oven, while *Poached Salmon with Watercress Sauce* requires a large pan for stove-top poaching. If you happen to have a special fish poaching pan, now is the time to use it, but a large roasting pan also works well. You will need a heavy casserole or large pot for stews and chowders, and frying  pans for sautéed and pan-fried fish dishes. For small whole fish, such as trout, you can find special oval fish pans, which are pretty enough to be taken to table, although a large frying pan can be substituted. Where specialty equipment is used I have suggested easy alternatives. For example, a steamer is called for in *Steamed Braided Fish with Warm Vinaigrette*, but a large pot with rack and lid can also be used. A deep-fat fryer is used in *Perfect Fish and Chips* but a shallow saucepan can be substituted.

INGREDIENTS

Fresh fish is delicious plainly cooked, but a variety of ingredients will bring out its individual flavor.

Lemon is a favorite partner, enhancing taste whether the fish is pan-fried, steamed, or baked. Other citrus fruits, such as orange and lime, also lend their acidity to fish with delicious results. A wide range of aromatic herbs complements fish, whether they form the basis of a sauce or are sprinkled on top before or after cooking. Onion, garlic, and shallot are essential to many fish dishes, while piquant flavorings, such as fresh hot chili pepper, fresh ginger root, and capers add their own distinctive tastes. Dried spices such as cayenne, cumin, coriander, cloves, saffron, and hot red pepper flakes are more unusual, but they enliven a surprising number of recipes. Coatings for fish range beyond the standard flour, beaten egg, and breadcrumbs. Rolled oats and sliced almonds also provide a tasty covering

for fillets. Batter for deep-frying includes a leavening of beer, and white wine forms the basis of half a dozen cooking liquids and sauces.

Shellfish are natural partners for fish. Shrimp and scallops combine with sole in *Seafood Lasagne*, while shrimp join haddock in *English Fish Pie*, and oysters and crayfish add authenticity to *Creole Bouillabaisse*. Mussels add zest to the cod in *New England Cod and Mussel Chowder*. Vegetables also play a leading role, whether as stuffing, garnish, or in a sauce. Tomatoes spring at once to mind: with their glowing color and touch of acid fruitiness they are ideal in sauces and salsas. Fennel is excellent with swordfish, while watercress is the perfect accompaniment to cold poached salmon. Spinach fills *Turbans of Sole with Spinach Mousse*, and acts as a background salad for *Tuna and Bacon Kebabs*, while mushrooms are essential to the classic *Sole Bonne Femme*.

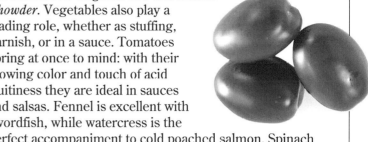

TECHNIQUES

A number of different techniques for preparing fish are illustrated in these recipes. Most importantly, you will learn how to prepare whole fish – how to scale them, clean them through the gills, fillet, skin, and trim them. The way to cut thin slices is illustrated, as well as how to cut up fish for soups and stews, and to purée it for a mousseline. You will also see the preparation of fish stock and court bouillon.

The recipes use a wide range of cooking methods, including poaching, broiling, and pan-frying, for whole fish, as well as fillets and smaller pieces. Tricky deep frying is carefully explained, and steaming instructions are given for fish pieces. Baking fish in a paper case is a more unusual approach illustrated here, and a seemingly complicated fish terrine is made simple with the step-by-step pictures. Knowing how to test when fish is done is vital because few foods overcook more easily. In each recipe you'll be given the correct procedure so you cannot go wrong, no matter if you are poaching, broiling, steaming, sautéing, deep-frying, or baking in the oven.

BROILED TUNA STEAKS WITH SALSA

🍽 SERVES 4   🥄 WORK TIME 25–30 MINUTES*   ♨ BROILING TIME 5–7 MINUTES

EQUIPMENT

non-metallic shallow dish

saucepans

citrus juicer   bowls

large metal spoon

pastry brush

slotted spoon

chef's knife

small knife

tongs

chopping board

paper towels

The intense heat of broiling is well-suited to rich fish such as tuna, searing the outside and keeping the inside moist. Here, a tart marinade made with lemon juice deliciously offsets the richness of the tuna. A crisp, fresh salsa of tomatoes, yellow corn, red bell peppers, and onion is the perfect foil.

GETTING AHEAD
The salsa can be made up to 1 day ahead and refrigerated. Broil the fish just before serving.
plus 1–2 hours marinating time

SHOPPING LIST

4	tuna steaks, weighing ½ lb each
	salt and pepper
4	medium tomatoes
2	ears of fresh corn or 1 cup defrosted corn kernels
1	medium red bell pepper
1	medium onion
1	medium bunch of fresh coriander (cilantro)
2	limes
3–4 tbsp	vegetable oil
	For the marinade
2–3	sprigs of fresh thyme
2 tbsp	vegetable oil
½	lemon

INGREDIENTS

tuna steaks †

fresh corn

red bell pepper

lemon

vegetable oil

limes

tomatoes

fresh thyme

onion

fresh coriander

† other suitable fish
monkfish, shark, swordfish

ORDER OF WORK

1 MARINATE THE TUNA

2 MAKE THE SALSA

3 BROIL THE TUNA

1 MARINATE THE TUNA

Sprinkle salt and pepper evenly over steaks

1 Strip the thyme leaves from the stems, letting them fall into the shallow dish. Add the oil to the dish.

2 Squeeze the juice from the lemon half and add the juice to the thyme and oil in the shallow dish.

3 Rinse the tuna steaks with cold water. Transfer to paper towels and pat dry. Season with salt and pepper. Put the tuna steaks into the marinade in the dish and turn them over, coating them well with the marinade. Cover and marinate 1–2 hours in the refrigerator, turning occasionally. While the fish is marinating, make the salsa.

2 MAKE THE SALSA

1 Cut the cores from the tomatoes and score an "x" on the base of each. Immerse them in a pan of boiling water until the skin starts to split. Transfer at once to a bowl of cold water. When cold, peel off the skin. Cut the tomatoes crosswise in half and squeeze out the seeds. Coarsely chop each half.

Skin splits in heat of water and makes peeling easy

2 Shuck the ears of corn: pull the husk down each ear to the base; trim off the husk and stem, then strip away the silky threads. Bring a large saucepan of water to a boil. Add the ears of corn to the pan, and cook them until tender, 5–7 minutes.

3 To test, lift 1 of the ears of corn out of the pan with the tongs. The kernels should pop out easily with the point of the small knife.

HOW TO CHOP AN ONION

The size of dice when chopping an onion depends on the thickness of the initial slices. For a standard size, make slices that are about ¹/₄ inch thick. For finely chopped onions, slice as thinly as possible.

1 Peel the onion and trim the top; leave a little of the root attached.

2 Cut the onion lengthwise in half, through root and stem.

3 Put one half, cut-side down, on the chopping board and hold the onion steady with one hand. Using a chef's knife, make a series of horizontal cuts from the top toward the root but not through it.

4 Make a series of lengthwise vertical cuts, cutting just to the root but not through it.

ANNE SAYS
"When slicing, tuck your fingertips under and use your knuckles to guide the blade of the knife."

5 Slice the onion crosswise into dice. For finely chopped onion, continue chopping until you have the fineness required.

Cut across at even intervals for neat dice

4 Drain the corn and let it cool slightly, then cut the kernels from the cobs. If using defrosted corn kernels, drain them.

Corn will add striking color and sweet taste to salsa

After boiling, corn kernels are easy to cut from cob

5 Core, seed, and dice the bell pepper (see box, page 14). Peel and chop the onion (see box, page 12).

Lime juice adds a Mexican touch

Salsa ingredients make brilliant color combination

6 Strip the coriander leaves from the stems and pile the leaves on the chopping board, reserving a few for decoration. Using the chef's knife, hold the tip of the blade against the board and rock the blade back and forth to finely chop the coriander leaves.

7 Put the chopped tomatoes, corn kernels, coriander, onion, and bell pepper in a bowl. Squeeze 1 of the limes and pour the juice into the salsa mixture. Add salt and pepper. Stir to combine the ingredients, then let stand 1 hour for the flavors to blend.

HOW TO CORE AND SEED A BELL PEPPER, AND CUT IT INTO DICE

The core and seeds of bell peppers must always be discarded.

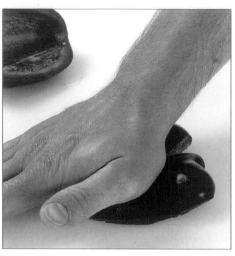

1 With a small knife, cut around the core of the bell pepper and pull it out. Halve the bell pepper lengthwise and scrape out the seeds. Cut away the white ribs on the inside of the pepper.

2 Set each pepper half cut-side down on the work surface and press down firmly with the heel of your hand on top of each pepper half to flatten.

3 With a chef's knife, slice the pepper half lengthwise into strips. To dice, gather the strips together in a pile and cut across into squares.

3 BROIL THE TUNA

ANNE SAYS
"If you like, you can grill the tuna on a charcoal grill; it will cook just as quickly."

1 Heat the broiler. Brush the broiler rack with oil. Put the tuna steaks on the broiler rack and brush with the marinade. Broil the steaks about 3 inches from the heat, 3–4 minutes.

Marinade on steaks gives tuna additional flavor

2 Turn over each tuna steak, using the tongs.

3 Brush with the remaining marinade and broil 2–3 minutes longer. The tuna should be brown on the outside, but still rare in the center. To test, flake with a knife: a translucent layer should be visible in the center.

ANNE SAYS
"*If grilling, you can make an attractive crosshatch pattern on the steaks. Cook 1–2 minutes until the grill marks show, then rotate the steaks 45° and continue grilling so the marks form diamonds.*"

4 Cut the second lime crosswise into thin slices with the chef's knife.

Slices of tangy lime echo salsa flavoring

🍴 **TO SERVE**
Arrange the tuna steaks on a bed of salsa on a platter and decorate each with a sprig of coriander. Arrange the lime slices around the tuna.

Fresh coriander decorates fish

Salsa adds cool freshness to broiled tuna

VARIATION
BROILED SWORDFISH WITH FENNEL AND SUN-DRIED TOMATOES

Here, swordfish steaks replace the tuna steaks. A mixture of pungent fennel, sun-dried tomatoes, and anise-flavored liqueur is the garnish.

1 Rinse and pat dry 4 swordfish steaks weighing 1/2 lb each, then marinate as directed. Omit the salsa.
2 Wash and trim 3 fennel bulbs. Cut them lengthwise in half and slice.
3 Melt 1/4 cup butter in a saucepan. Add the fennel, season with a little salt and pepper, and press a piece of buttered foil on top. Put on the lid and cook over low heat, stirring occasionally, until very soft, 40–45 minutes.
4 Drain 1/2 cup sun-dried tomatoes packed in oil and coarsely chop them. Stir them into the fennel with 1–2 tbsp anise-flavored liqueur. Continue cooking the mixture about 10 minutes, then season to taste with salt and pepper.
5 Broil the swordfish steaks as directed for the tuna steaks, and serve on warmed individual plates with the fennel mixture on the side.

CRISP-SIDED SALMON WITH FRESH CORIANDER PESTO

🍴 SERVES 4   🥣 WORK TIME 5–10 MINUTES   ♨ COOKING TIME 10–15 MINUTES

EQUIPMENT

food processor

rubber spatula

pastry brush

tweezers

chef's knife

filleting knife

metal spatula

bowls

paper towels

large frying pan, preferably cast iron

cheese grater

chopping board

This is a newly popular method for cooking fish: fillets are fried until crispy on the skin side, and only lightly cooked on the top. Rich fish such as salmon and sea bass are particularly suitable for cooking in this way. Pesto made with fresh coriander (cilantro) is the perfect partner.

GETTING AHEAD

The pesto can be made up to 48 hours ahead and kept, covered, in the refrigerator; it can also be frozen. The salmon should be cooked just before serving.

SHOPPING LIST

4	pieces of fresh salmon fillet, with skin, weighing about 6 oz each
3 tbsp	vegetable oil
1	lemon
2 tsp	coarse salt
	coriander leaves
	For the fresh coriander pesto
1	large bunch of fresh coriander (cilantro)
2–3	garlic cloves
2 tbsp	pine nuts
⅓ cup	olive oil
¼ cup	grated Parmesan cheese
	salt and pepper

INGREDIENTS

fresh salmon fillet †

Parmesan cheese   fresh coriander

pine nuts

olive oil   vegetable oil

garlic cloves

lemon   coarse salt

† other suitable fish

bluefish, mackerel, red snapper, salmon trout, sea bass

ORDER OF WORK

1   **MAKE THE FRESH CORIANDER PESTO**

2   **PREPARE AND COOK THE SALMON**

1 MAKE THE FRESH CORIANDER PESTO

1 Put the coriander leaves in the food processor with the garlic, pine nuts, and 2 tbsp olive oil. Add the cheese.

2 With the blade of the food processor turning, slowly pour in the remaining olive oil in a thin, steady stream.

Coriander leaves for pesto are stripped from stems

3 Continue working the ingredients in the machine until the pesto thickens and emulsifies. Season to taste with salt and pepper.

2 PREPARE AND COOK THE SALMON

1 If necessary, pull out any pin bones from the pieces of salmon fillet with the tweezers.

2 Cut off any fatty or bony edges from the pieces of salmon. Trim the pieces neatly.

Salmon must be thoroughly dry before cooking

3 Rinse the pieces of salmon under cold running water. Transfer them to paper towels and pat dry.

Place fish skin-side down on paper towels

4 Transfer to a plate and brush the skin side of each piece of salmon fillet with some of the vegetable oil.

5 Heat the remaining oil in the frying pan until it is hot. Add the salmon fillets to the pan, placing them skin-side down.

†⊙† TO SERVE
Transfer the salmon fillets to warmed individual plates, sprinkle with the coarse salt, and spoon some coriander pesto beside each fillet. Decorate with twisted lemon slices and coriander leaves.

Pink salmon contrasts in both taste and color with green pesto

6 Cook over medium heat until the skin is quite crispy and the sides are opaque, 10–15 minutes, depending on the thickness of the fillets. The top should be still slightly soft, showing that it is rare. Meanwhile, slice the lemon for decoration.

ANNE SAYS
"If you prefer your salmon fully cooked, cover the pan, and continue cooking 1–2 minutes."

V A R I A T I O N
CRISP-SIDED SALMON WITH GARLIC SABAYON
The sabayon here is made in the same way as a Hollandaise sauce
with the addition of a garlic and wine flavoring.

1 To make the sauce, peel and chop 2 shallots (see box, below). Peel and chop 4 garlic cloves. Melt 1 tbsp butter in a pan, add the shallots and garlic. Cook until soft, 3–5 minutes.

2 Add 1 tbsp heavy cream; bring to a boil. Add ¼ cup each of white wine and sweet vermouth. Cook over high heat until reduced to 2–3 tbsp. Let cool slightly.

3 Melt ½ cup butter; skim off the froth. Let cool to tepid.

4 Put 2 egg yolks and 2 tbsp water in a heatproof bowl; whisk until light in color. Set over a pan of hot water; whisk until the mixture is thick enough to leave a ribbon trail, 5 minutes.

5 Take the bowl from the pan of water; whisk in the butter in a slow, steady stream, leaving the milk solids from the butter at the bottom of the pan. Whisk in the garlic mixture. Season to taste with salt, white pepper, and a squeeze of lemon juice. Keep warm by setting the bowl in a pan of warm water.

6 Cook the salmon as directed; transfer to warmed individual plates. Heat the broiler.

7 Spoon the garlic sabayon onto the salmon fillets to coat them. Broil about 4 inches from the heat until the sabayon is lightly browned, 1–2 minutes. Serve immediately.

HOW TO CHOP A SHALLOT

For a standard chop, make slices that are about ⅛ inch thick.
For a fine chop, make the slices as thin as possible.

1 Peel the outer, papery skin from the shallot. Separate the shallot into sections if necessary.

2 Set a section flat side down on a chopping board. Holding the shallot steady, slice horizontally, leaving the slices attached at the root.

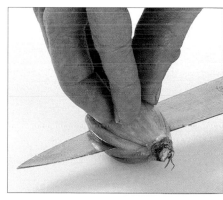

3 Slice vertically through the shallot, again leaving the root end uncut.

Cut just to root so shallot holds together

Sharp chef's knife makes slicing easy

4 Cut across into fine dice. Continue chopping until very fine, if necessary, holding the tip of the blade and rocking it up and down.

SPICY FISH STEW

 SERVES 6   WORK TIME 30–35 MINUTES   COOKING TIME 30–35 MINUTES

EQUIPMENT

flameproof casserole with lid

cheesecloth †

paper towels

saucepans, 1 with lid

wooden spoon

small knife

slotted spoon

filleting knife

bowls

chef's knife

vegetable peeler

apple corer

strainer

chopping board

†dish towel can also be used

This tasty casserole, flavored with apple, coconut, and spices, is delicious accompanied by poppadums. Serve boiled rice on the side.

SHOPPING LIST

2 lb	skinned monkfish fillets
6	medium tomatoes, total weight about 2 lb
2	medium carrots
2	celery stalks
6	garlic cloves
2	medium onions
1/4 cup	vegetable oil
2 tbsp	paprika
1 1/4 cups	fish stock (see box, page 124)
4	bay leaves
	salt and pepper
	For the spicy sauce
1 1/4 cups	fish stock
1 1/2 cups	unsweetened shredded coconut
1	medium onion
1	medium apple
2 tbsp	butter
1 tsp	ground cumin
1 tsp	ground coriander
1/2 tsp	ground ginger
1/2 tsp	ground cloves
1/4 tsp	cayenne or 1/2 tsp hot red pepper flakes
1 1/2 tbsp	cornstarch

INGREDIENTS

monkfish fillets †

bay leaves

apple

onions

ground cloves

ground cumin

vegetable oil

garlic cloves

unsweetened shredded coconut

butter

tomatoes

fish stock

celery

carrots

ground coriander

paprika

cayenne

cornstarch

ground ginger

† other suitable fish

grouper, mahi mahi, orange roughy, red snapper, shark

ORDER OF WORK

1 MAKE THE SPICY SAUCE

2 PREPARE THE MONKFISH AND VEGETABLES

3 COOK THE FISH STEW

20

1 MAKE THE SPICY SAUCE

1 Bring the fish stock to a boil in a medium saucepan. Add the shredded coconut.

2 Stir to mix, then cover the pan and leave the coconut to soak 30 minutes.

ANNE SAYS
"As the coconut soaks, the stock will become infused with its flavor, making coconut milk."

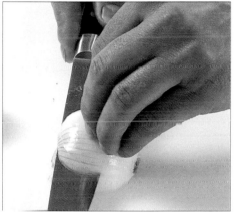

Lay each onion half flat on chopping board for dicing

Curled fingers guide knife

3 Peel the onion, leaving a little root attached, and cut lengthwise in half. Slice each half horizontally toward the root, leaving the slices attached.

4 Slice each onion half vertically, again leaving the root end uncut, then cut across to make dice.

Transfer coconut to cheesecloth to finely strain

5 Put a large piece of cheesecloth in the strainer, set over a bowl. Spoon in the coconut and its liquid.

6 Gather up the ends of the cheesecloth and squeeze the coconut well to extract as much liquid or "milk" as possible. Discard the coconut and wipe the saucepan.

7 Peel the apple and core it with the apple corer. Cut the apple into halves. Cut each half horizontally into ³/₈-inch slices, then cut lengthwise into strips. Cut across into dice.

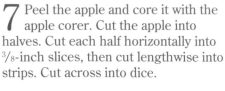

Hold apple half together with fingers as you cut

Apple strips are easy to cut into dice

8 Melt the butter in the saucepan. Add the onion and apple, and cook until soft but not brown, 3–5 minutes.

9 Add the ground cumin, coriander, ginger, cloves, and cayenne to the onion and apple. Cook, stirring, over low heat, 2–3 minutes.

Paste of cornstarch and coconut milk slightly thickens stew

Stir sauce constantly while adding cornstarch paste

10 Put the cornstarch in a small bowl. Add 2–3 tbsp of the coconut milk and blend to a smooth paste. Add remaining coconut milk to the saucepan and bring to a boil.

11 Stir in the cornstarch paste; the sauce will thicken at once. Take the pan from the heat and season the sauce to taste with salt and pepper. Set aside.

ANNE SAYS
"If the cornstarch forms lumps, stir vigorously to dissolve them."

2 PREPARE THE MONKFISH AND VEGETABLES

1 With the filleting knife, cut away the membrane from the monkfish. Rinse the monkfish with cold water and pat dry with paper towels.

Membrane on monkfish must always be completely removed

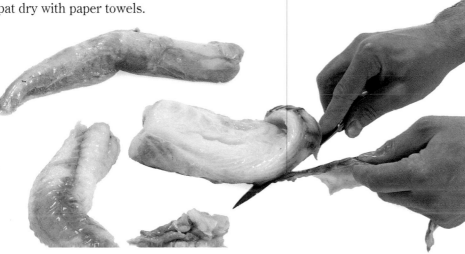

2 Cut the monkfish fillets into 1-inch strips, then across into cubes. Set aside while preparing the vegetables.

3 Cut the cores from the tomatoes and score an "x" on the base of each with the tip of a knife. Immerse in a pan of boiling water until the skin starts to split, 8–15 seconds depending on ripeness. Using the slotted spoon, transfer at once to cold water. When cold, peel off the skin. Cut crosswise in half and squeeze out the seeds, then coarsely chop each half.

4 Peel the carrots and trim them. Cut them across into thin slices using the chef's knife.

5 Peel the strings from the celery stalks, then cut the stalks across into thin slices.

Run peeler up celery stalks to remove tough strings

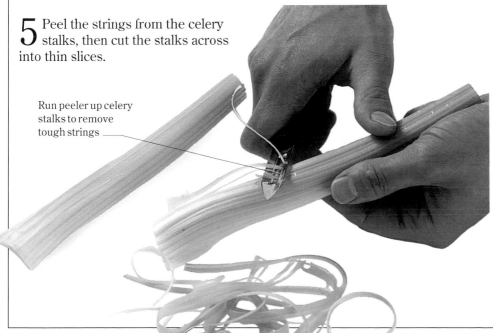

6 Set the flat side of the chef's knife on top of each garlic clove and strike it with your fist. Discard the skin and finely chop the garlic. Peel the onions, leaving a little of the root attached, and cut them in half through root and stem. Cut each onion half across into thin slices.

3 COOK THE FISH STEW

1 Heat the oil in the casserole. Add the onions and cook until soft but not brown, 3–5 minutes.

Metal spoon is preferable to wooden spoon because it does not absorb spices

Paprika adds deep color to fried onions

2 Add the paprika and cook, about 1 minute, stirring to combine evenly with the onions.

Carrot slices will keep shape and color in stew

3 Add the fish stock, chopped tomatoes, garlic, bay leaves, celery, and carrots to the casserole with a little salt and pepper. Bring the mixture to a boil.

4 Reduce the heat and simmer until the liquid is reduced by one-third, 15–20 minutes.

5 Add the spicy sauce to the casserole and stir well, then bring back to a boil.

6 Add the fish. Cover and simmer, stirring occasionally, until the fish flakes easily, 12–15 minutes. Discard the bay leaves and taste for seasoning.

¶◯§ TO SERVE
Serve the spicy fish stew in individual warmed bowls.

Crisp poppadums
perfectly complement
this spicy dish

Fish stew flavored
with rich mix of
spices is delicious
and warming meal

VARIATION
SPICY FISH STEW WITH POTATOES

1 Make the spicy sauce as directed in the main recipe, omitting the apple.
2 Prepare the vegetables as directed, omitting the carrots and celery.
3 Peel 2 medium potatoes and cut them into rough chunks.
4 Omit the monkfish and prepare the same weight of skinned grouper or haddock fillets.
5 Cook the fish stew as directed, adding the potatoes and 1 cup fresh or defrosted green peas with the tomatoes. Continue cooking the stew as directed. Add the fish and simmer as directed in the main recipe, 12–15 minutes.
6 Serve in individual warmed bowls sprinkled with coarsely chopped unsalted peanuts.

VARIATION
SPICY FISH STEW WITH BELL PEPPERS

1 Make the spicy sauce as directed in the main recipe, omitting the apple.
2 Prepare the vegetables as directed, omitting the carrots and celery.
3 Cut out the core from 1 green, 1 red, and 1 yellow bell pepper, then halve the peppers and scrape out the seeds. Cut away the white ribs on the inside. Set each pepper half cut-side down on the chopping board and press with the heel of your hand to flatten it. Slice it lengthwise into medium strips.
4 Omit the monkfish and prepare the same weight of skinned grouper or haddock fillets.
5 Cook the fish stew as directed, adding the bell pepper slices with the tomatoes. Add the fish and simmer as directed, 12–15 minutes.
6 Chop a few fresh chives and sprinkle over the stew before serving.

GETTING AHEAD
The fish stew can be made up to 1 day ahead and kept refrigerated. Reheat it on top of the stove before serving.

ORIENTAL HALIBUT IN A PAPER CASE

EQUIPMENT

parchment paper

pencil

paper towels

pastry brush

chef's knife

small knife

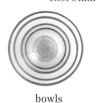
bowls

strainer

kitchen scissors

colander

baking sheet

saucepan

chopping board

This recipe combines Chinese flavorings with a French cooking method. Topped with black beans and soy sauce, the fish is baked in individual paper cases. Each diner opens a paper case and savors the aroma. Cellophane noodles and stir-fried vegetables would be ideal accompaniments.

GETTING AHEAD
The filled paper cases can be prepared up to 4 hours in advance and refrigerated. Bake just before serving.

SHOPPING LIST

¼ lb	snow peas
1-inch	piece of fresh ginger root
4	garlic cloves
4	scallions
¼ cup	fermented black beans
3 tbsp	light soy sauce
2 tbsp	dry sherry
½ tsp	sugar
1 tbsp	sesame oil
2 tbsp	vegetable oil
4	skinned halibut fillets or steaks, weighing about 6 oz each
	For the egg glaze
1	egg
½ tsp	salt

INGREDIENTS

halibut fillets†

fermented black beans

sesame oil

scallions

light soy sauce

sugar

egg

fresh ginger root

dry sherry

vegetable oil

snow peas

garlic cloves

† other suitable fish
cod, grouper, John Dory, orange roughy

ORDER OF WORK

1 PREPARE THE VEGETABLES AND ORIENTAL SEASONING

2 PREPARE THE PAPER CASES

3 FILL AND BAKE THE PAPER CASES

1 PREPARE THE VEGETABLES AND ORIENTAL SEASONING

1 Trim the stem end from each snow pea and pull the string down the pod. Trim the other end.

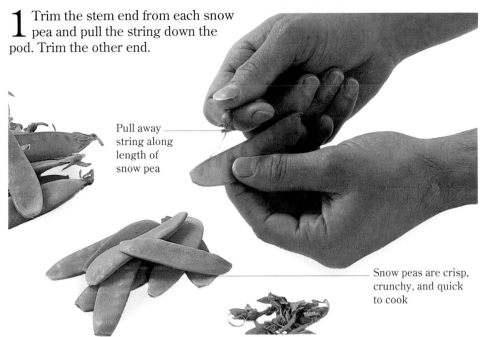

Pull away string along length of snow pea

Snow peas are crisp, crunchy, and quick to cook

2 Half-fill the saucepan with salted water and bring to a boil. Add the snow peas and simmer 1–2 minutes. Drain in the colander, rinse with cold water, and drain again.

3 With the small knife, peel the skin from the ginger root. With the chef's knife, slice the ginger, cutting across the fibrous grain. Crush the slices of ginger with the flat of the knife, then finely chop them.

4 Set the flat side of the chef's knife on top of each garlic clove and strike it with your fist. Discard the skin and finely chop the garlic.

5 Trim the scallions. Cut them into thin diagonal slices, including some of the green tops.

6 Put the fermented black beans in the strainer, rinse with cold water, and drain thoroughly. Reserve one-quarter of the whole beans and coarsely chop the rest.

Sesame oil is essential flavor in oriental seasoning

7 Combine the garlic, ginger, chopped and whole black beans, soy sauce, sherry, sugar, and sesame oil in a bowl. Stir the oriental seasoning well to mix, then set aside.

2 PREPARE THE PAPER CASES

1 Fold a large sheet of parchment paper (about 12 x 15 inches) in half and draw a curve to make a heart shape when unfolded. It should be large enough to leave a 3-inch border around a halibut fillet.

2 Cut out the heart shape, cutting just inside the drawn line. Repeat to make a total of 4 paper hearts.

ANNE SAYS
"Aluminum foil can be used instead of paper, but it will not puff and brown."

3 Open out each paper heart and brush with the vegetable oil, leaving a border about 1 inch wide. For the glaze, beat the egg with the salt until mixed. Brush the egg glaze on the border of each paper heart.

3 FILL AND BAKE THE PAPER CASES

1 Heat the oven to 400° F. Rinse the fish fillets and pat dry with paper towels. Arrange one-quarter of the snow peas on one side of each paper heart and set a fish fillet on top.

2 Spoon one-quarter of the oriental seasoning on top of each fillet and sprinkle with one-quarter of the scallions.

Scallions will keep crispness when cooked this way

3 Fold the paper over the fish and run your finger along the edge to stick the 2 sides of each paper heart together. Make small pleats to seal the edges of each paper case.

4 Twist the "tails" of each paper case to seal them so that the filling does not ooze out during baking.

Steam from cooked
fish puffs paper packages

5 Lay the
paper cases
on the baking sheet.
Bake them in the heated
oven until puffed and
brown, 10–12 minutes.

🍴 **TO SERVE**
Transfer the puffed paper cases to
warmed individual plates, so that
each person can open a paper case.
If the paper cases cool and deflate
before serving, warm them briefly
in the oven to puff them again.

Paper cases
enclose
wonderful
aromas

VARIATION

THAI-STYLE HALIBUT IN A PAPER CASE

1 Omit the snow peas and the
oriental seasoning.
2 Put ³/₄ oz dried Chinese black
mushrooms in a bowl of warm water
and soak them until plump, about
30 minutes. Drain and slice if large.
3 Finely chop the fresh ginger root
and 2 garlic cloves as directed in the
main recipe. Slice 2 scallions.
4 Cut 1 fresh hot green chili pepper
lengthwise in half, discarding the core.
Scrape out the seeds and cut away the
fleshy white ribs from each half. Cut
each half into very thin strips, then
cut across to produce very fine dice.
5 Strip the leaves from 5 sprigs of
fresh basil. Peel and slice 1 lime.
Squeeze the juice from a second lime.
6 Put the mushrooms, garlic,
1 tbsp soy sauce, 1 tsp sugar, and
¹/₂ cup water in a small saucepan
and boil until all the liquid has
evaporated, 5–7 minutes. Stir in
the ginger, chili pepper, basil
leaves, 2 tsp fish sauce (nam pla),
and the lime juice.
7 Prepare the paper cases and fish
as directed. Spoon the mushroom
mixture over the fish, then sprinkle
with the sliced scallions. Put a lime
slice on top and season with pepper.
Fold the paper over, close the cases
and bake as directed.
8 If you like, accompany each
serving with a fine ribbon pasta,
decorated with shredded basil and
diced mushroom.

TUNA AND BACON KEBABS

EQUIPMENT

whisk

small knife

pastry brush

chef's knife

colander

paper towels

8 long metal skewers

bowls

chopping board

ANNE SAYS
"You could use bamboo skewers, instead of the metal ones suggested here, but cover them with water and soak 30 minutes first."

Chunks of tuna are steeped in a tart marinade, then wrapped in slices of bacon and threaded onto skewers with cherry tomatoes to be quickly broiled. A salad of spinach and mango creates a tropical presentation.

GETTING AHEAD

The tuna can be marinated and the salad and dressing prepared up to 4 hours ahead; keep the fish and salad in the refrigerator. Assemble and broil the kebabs and toss the salad just before serving.

* plus 30–60 minutes marinating time

SHOPPING LIST

2 1/2 lb	skinned tuna fillet or steak
1 lb	cherry tomatoes
1 lb	thick-cut bacon
	vegetable oil for skewers and broiler rack
	salt and pepper
For the marinade	
1/3 cup	lime juice, from 2 limes
2 tbsp	olive oil
	Tabasco sauce
For the spinach and mango salad	
1/2 lb	spinach leaves
1	ripe mango
	juice of 1 lime
1/4 tsp	Dijon-style mustard
1/3 cup	vegetable oil

INGREDIENTS

tuna fillet †

bacon

cherry tomatoes

spinach leaves

vegetable oil

Dijon-style mustard

lime juice

olive oil

mango

Tabasco sauce

† other suitable fish
cod, grouper, swordfish, shark

ORDER OF WORK

1 PREPARE AND MARINATE THE TUNA

2 PREPARE THE SALAD AND DRESSING

3 ASSEMBLE AND BROIL THE KEBABS; TOSS THE SALAD

1 PREPARE AND MARINATE THE TUNA

1 Rinse the tuna with cold water and pat dry with paper towels. Cut the fish lengthwise into 1¹/₂ inch strips, then cut the strips crosswise into cubes.

Slice tuna into strips first to make neat cubes

Cut strips into even chunks, so they cook at same speed

2 Make the marinade: whisk the lime juice with the olive oil, a dash of Tabasco sauce, and a little salt and pepper in a large non-metallic bowl.

3 Add the cubes of tuna and toss until they are well coated with the marinade. Cover and marinate 30–60 minutes in the refrigerator.

2 PREPARE THE SALAD AND DRESSING

Blot all water from spinach leaves

1 Remove the tough ribs and stems from the spinach leaves, pulling them away with your fingers.

2 Wash the spinach leaves thoroughly and pat dry in a dish towel.

3 Peel the mango with the small knife. Cut lengthwise into 2 pieces, slightly off center so the knife just misses the pit. Cut the flesh away from the other side of the pit.

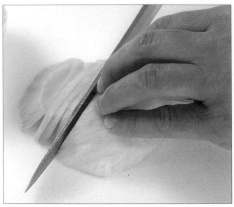

4 Cut the pieces of mango flesh into neat slices. Cut the remaining mango flesh away from the pit and neatly slice, then discard the pit.

5 Make the dressing: in a small bowl whisk the lime juice with the mustard, salt, and pepper. Gradually whisk in the oil so the dressing emulsifies. Taste for seasoning.

3 ASSEMBLE AND BROIL THE KEBABS; TOSS THE SALAD

1 Put the cherry tomatoes in the colander and rinse under cold running water. Transfer the tomatoes to paper towels to dry.

Spread out cherry tomatoes on paper towels so they will be dry before broiling

2 Cut the bacon slices crosswise in half (each piece should be about $2^{1}/_{2}$ inches long). Heat the broiler. Brush the metal skewers and the broiler rack with oil.

Bacon wrapping helps keep tuna moist and juicy

3 Wrap a piece of bacon around each cube of tuna. Thread the bacon-wrapped fish onto the skewers, alternating the fish with the cherry tomatoes.

! TAKE CARE !
Do not pack the ingredients too tightly on the skewers or they will not cook evenly.

4 Set the assembled kebabs on the prepared broiler rack, in 2 batches if necessary, and broil the kebabs about 3 inches from the heat until the bacon is crisp and golden, 5–6 minutes. Turn the kebabs and continue broiling until the bacon is crisp and brown and the fish is cooked through, 5–6 minutes longer.

Arrange mango slices attractively

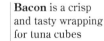

5 Meanwhile, toss the spinach leaves with three-quarters of the dressing. Spread the spinach on 8 individual plates and arrange the mango slices on top. Sprinkle with the remaining dressing.

🍴 **TO SERVE**
Place a broiled tuna and bacon kebab across the center of the spinach leaves on each plate.

Bacon is a crisp and tasty wrapping for tuna cubes

Spinach makes a tender bed for kebabs

V A R I A T I O N

MONKFISH AND BACON KEBABS

Chunks of monkfish wrapped in bacon alternate with red onions to make up the kebabs.

1 Replace the tuna with the same weight of monkfish fillet. Cut away the thin membrane covering the outside of the monkfish, then cut the fish into cubes and marinate as directed.
2 Prepare the spinach and dressing as directed; omit the mango.
3 Clean and slice 1/4 lb mushrooms.
4 Cut 2 avocados in half, discard the pits, and peel off the skin. Cut the avocado halves lengthwise into strips and sprinkle them thoroughly with the juice of 1 lime.
5 Peel 4 small red onions and cut each into wedges, leaving a little of the root to hold the wedges together.
6 Wrap the monkfish cubes in bacon and thread them onto the skewers, alternating with the onion wedges. Broil the kebabs as directed.
7 Meanwhile, toss the spinach in three-quarters of the dressing, arrange on individual plates, and top with the mushroom slices and avocado strips. Sprinkle the salad with the remaining dressing.
8 Slide the bacon-wrapped fish and the onions off the skewers and arrange on the salad. Serve immediately.

NEW ENGLAND COD AND MUSSEL CHOWDER

 SERVES 8   WORK TIME 45–50 MINUTES   COOKING TIME 55–60 MINUTES

EQUIPMENT

small knife

chef's knife

stiff brush

large saucepan

colander

vegetable peeler

wooden spoon

paper towels

bowls

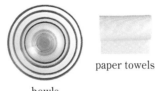
large casserole

chopping board

A hearty white fish stew, this chowder is laden with chunks of cod and potatoes, with mussels in their shells to add color and flavor. At the end of cooking, some of the potatoes are crushed to thicken the chowder. Oyster crackers are the traditional accompaniment.

GETTING AHEAD

The chowder can be made through step 7 up to 2 days ahead and kept, covered, in the refrigerator. Prepare the mussels and cod and finish the chowder just before serving.

SHOPPING LIST

2	medium onions
2	celery stalks
1	medium carrot
3	medium potatoes, total weight about 1 lb
5–7	sprigs of fresh dill
6 oz	sliced bacon
2 lb	skinned cod fillets
1 quart	mussels
1½ quarts	fish stock (see box, page 124)
2	bay leaves
½ cup	white wine
2 tsp	dried thyme
¼ cup	flour
1 cup	heavy cream
	salt and pepper

INGREDIENTS

cod fillets †

mussels

potatoes

fresh dill

onions

celery

bay leaves

sliced bacon

carrot

flour

dried thyme

heavy cream

white wine

fish stock

†other suitable fish
haddock, hake, pollack

ORDER OF WORK

1 PREPARE THE CHOWDER INGREDIENTS

2 MAKE THE CHOWDER

1 PREPARE THE CHOWDER INGREDIENTS

1 Peel the onions, leaving a little of the root attached, and cut them in half through root and stem. Slice each half horizontally toward the root, leaving the slices attached at the root end, then slice vertically, again leaving the root end uncut. Finally, cut across the onion to make dice.

Crunchy celery will become soft and tender when simmered

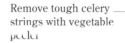

Remove tough celery strings with vegetable peeler

2 Peel the strings from the celery stalks. Cut each stalk lengthwise into ¼-inch strips, then gather the strips together into a pile and cut crosswise into small dice. Peel the carrot and dice into ¼-inch cubes (see box, below).

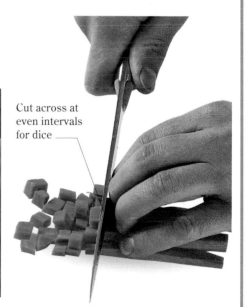

HOW TO DICE VEGETABLES

Root vegetables, such as carrots, turnips, and potatoes, are often diced before cooking. The size of the dice depends on the thickness of the initial slices.

Cut across at even intervals for dice

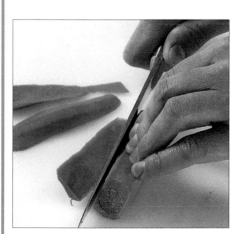

1 After peeling or trimming the vegetable, if necessary square off the sides, using a chef's knife to achieve a neat finish.

2 Cut the vegetable vertically into slices of the specified thickness. Stack the slices on the chopping board and cut them into strips of the specified thickness.

3 Gather the strips together into a pile and cut them crosswise to produce even dice.

Cold water
prevents diced
potatoes from
discoloring

3 Peel and dice the
potatoes into 1/2-inch
cubes (see box, page 35).
Put in cold water so they
do not discolor.

4 Strip the dill leaves from the stems
and pile them on the chopping
board. With the chef's knife, coarsely
chop the leaves and set aside for
decoration of the finished dish.

5 Stack the bacon slices on the
chopping board and cut across into
strips, then chop the strips into dice.

6 Rinse the cod fillets with cold water
and pat them dry with paper
towels. Remove any bones and cut the
fillets into 1-inch strips, then across
into 1-inch cubes. Prepare the mussels
(see box, page 37).

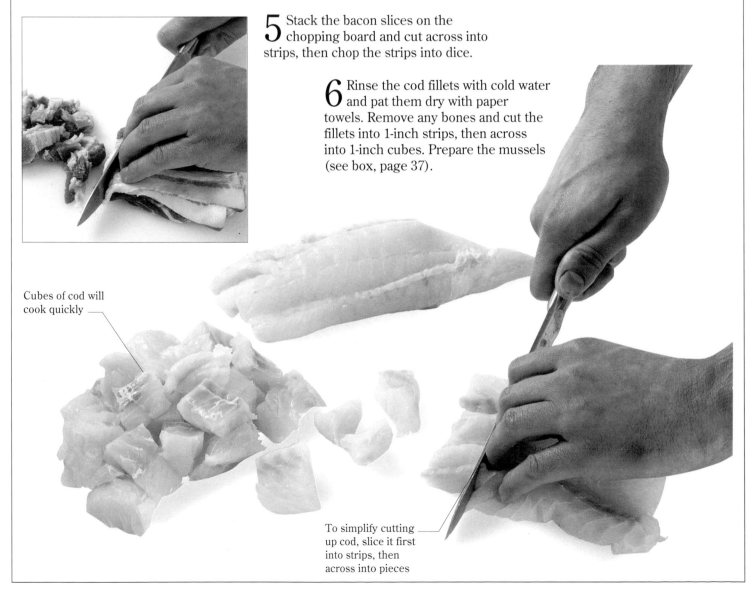

Cubes of cod will
cook quickly

To simplify cutting
up cod, slice it first
into strips, then
across into pieces

HOW TO PREPARE MUSSELS

Before cooking, mussels must be carefully scraped and washed to remove barnacles, sand, and the "beard" that attaches them to the stakes on which they grow.

1 With a small knife, detach and discard any weed or "beard" from the mussels. Scrape each mussel to remove any barnacles.

! TAKE CARE !
Discard any mussels that have broken shells or that do not close when tapped.

2 Scrub the mussels thoroughly under cold running water using a stiff brush.

2 MAKE THE CHOWDER

White wine adds acidity to chowder

Aromatic bay leaves give depth of flavor to chowder

1 Put the fish stock and bay leaves in the pan and pour in the wine. Heat the stock mixture to boiling and simmer 10 minutes.

ANNE SAYS
"For the fish stock, you can substitute two-thirds the amount bottled clam juice and one-third water."

2 Meanwhile, put the bacon in the casserole and cook, stirring occasionally, until crisp and the fat is rendered (melted), 3–5 minutes.

3 Add the diced onions, celery, carrot, and thyme. Cook, stirring, until the vegetables are soft but not brown, 5–7 minutes.

Flour helps to thicken chowder

4 Sprinkle the flour over the bacon and vegetables in the casserole and cook, stirring, 1 minute.

Stir to distribute flour evenly

5 Add the hot stock mixture to the vegetables and bring to a boil, stirring until the liquid boils and thickens slightly.

6 Drain the potatoes and add them to the casserole. Simmer, stirring occasionally, until the potatoes are very tender, about 40 minutes.

7 Remove the casserole from the heat. Using a fork, crush about one-third of the potatoes against the side of the casserole, then stir to combine.

ANNE SAYS
"The crushed potatoes help thicken the chowder."

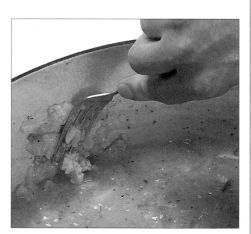

Tip in cleaned mussels all at once

Mussels will open quickly in heat of chowder

8 Return the casserole to the heat. Add the mussels to the chowder and simmer until the shells start to open, 1–2 minutes.

9 Stir in the cubed cod and simmer the chowder until the fish just flakes easily, 2–3 minutes longer.

10 Pour in the heavy cream and bring just to a boil. Taste the chowder for seasoning.

TO SERVE
Discard the bay leaves and any mussels that have not opened. Ladle the chowder into soup bowls and sprinkle each serving with the chopped dill. Serve very hot with oyster crackers to sprinkle over the stew.

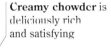

Creamy chowder is deliciously rich and satisfying

VARIATION

MANHATTAN COD AND MUSSEL CHOWDER

Manhattan chowder adds tomatoes, tomato paste, and garlic for a colorful finish.

1 Prepare the chowder ingredients as directed in the main recipe.

2 Cut the cores from 2½ lb tomatoes and score an "x" on the base of each with the tip of a knife. Immerse them in a pan of boiling water until the skin starts to split, 8–15 seconds depending on their ripeness. Using a slotted spoon, transfer them at once to a bowl of cold water. When cold, peel off the skin. Cut the tomatoes crosswise in half and squeeze out the seeds, then coarsely chop each half. Alternatively, use 3 cups canned tomatoes.

3 Peel 4 garlic cloves: set the flat side of the chef's knife on top of each clove and strike it with your fist. Discard the skin and finely chop the garlic.

4 Make the chowder as directed, using double the amount of white wine, 1 tbsp dried thyme, and half the amount of flour. Add the chopped garlic and 1–2 tbsp tomato paste with the onions, celery, and carrots. Add the chopped tomatoes with the potatoes; do not crush any of the potatoes. Omit the heavy cream.

5 Sprinkle with chopped thyme and serve the chowder with crusty whole wheat bread if you like.

PERFECT FISH AND CHIPS

🍴 SERVES 4   🥣 WORK TIME 45–50 MINUTES*   🍲 DEEP-FRYING TIME 20–25 MINUTES

EQUIPMENT

deep-fat fryer with thermostat

wooden spoon

vegetable peeler   small knife

bowls   paper towels

chef's knife

whisk †   colander

2-pronged fork

baking sheet   chopping board

† electric mixer can also be used

ANNE SAYS
"If you have no thermostat with your fryer, drop in a cube of fresh bread to test the temperature; if it turns golden brown in 60 seconds, the oil is at about 350°F, if it is golden brown in 40 seconds the oil is at about 375°F."

This quintessential British favorite features cod deep-fried in a light beer batter. For crispness, the chips (British for French fries) are deep-fried twice: first to cook them, then to brown them. The traditional accompaniment is tartare sauce.

GETTING AHEAD
The fish and batter can be prepared, and the chips given one deep-frying, up to 2 hours ahead. Deep-fry the fish and brown the chips just before serving so they will be crisp.

*plus 30–35 minutes standing time

SHOPPING LIST

6	medium potatoes, total weight about 1½ lb
	vegetable oil for deep-frying
1½ lb	skinned cod fillets
1	lemon
¼ cup	flour
	salt and pepper
	For the batter
1½ tsp	active dry yeast or ½ cake (9 g) compressed yeast
¼ cup	warm water
1¼ cups	flour
1 tbsp	vegetable oil
¾ cup	beer
1	egg white
	tartare sauce (see box, page 43) for serving (optional)

INGREDIENTS

cod fillets †

lemon

vegetable oil

potatoes

egg white

oil for deep-frying

beer

active dry yeast

flour

†other suitable fish
catfish, haddock, hake, flounder, perch

ORDER OF WORK

1 PREPARE THE POTATOES AND BATTER

2 PART-FRY THE CHIPS AND PREPARE THE FISH

3 COAT AND DEEP-FRY THE FISH; BROWN THE CHIPS

1 PREPARE THE POTATOES AND BATTER

Slice evenly for
neat sticks

1 Using the vegetable peeler, peel the potatoes. With the chef's knife, square off the sides and ends of each potato.

2 Cut each potato lengthwise into ³/₈-inch slices, guiding the knife against your curled fingers as you slice.

3 Stack the slices and cut them into ³/₈-inch sticks. Put them in a bowl of cold water to soak 30 minutes.

ANNE SAYS
"Soaking removes starch so the potatoes will be crisp when deep-fried."

Beer in yeast
batter helps it
froth

4 Meanwhile, sprinkle or crumble the yeast over the warm water and let stand until the yeast has dissolved, about 5 minutes.

5 Sift the flour and a pinch of salt into a large bowl and make a well in the center. Add the yeast mixture, the oil, and two-thirds of the beer; stir with a wooden spoon to form a smooth paste. Stir in the remaining beer.

! TAKE CARE !
Do not overmix or the batter will become too elastic.

6 Let the batter stand in a warm place 30–35 minutes until it has thickened and become frothy, showing the yeast is working, as above right.

2 PART-FRY THE CHIPS AND PREPARE THE FISH

1 While the batter is standing, heat the vegetable oil in the deep-fat fryer to 350°F. Drain the potatoes, transfer to paper towels, and pat dry.

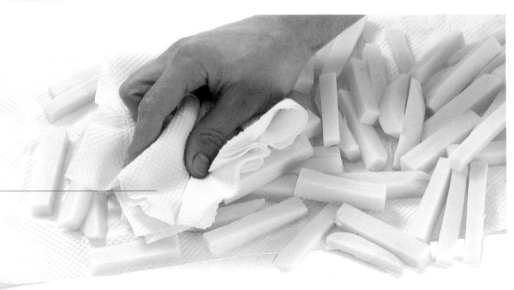

Dry potatoes thoroughly: any water left on them will make hot oil spit

After first deep-frying, potatoes should be just tender

2 Dip the empty frying basket in the hot oil (this will prevent the potatoes from sticking to it). Lift the basket out of the oil and add the potatoes. Carefully lower the basket back into the oil and deep-fry until the potatoes are just tender when pierced with the tip of the small knife, and are just starting to brown, 5–7 minutes. Lift out the basket and let the potatoes drain over the deep fryer, then tip them onto a plate lined with paper towels.

! TAKE CARE !
Do not overfill the basket or the oil could bubble over. Deep-fry the potatoes in batches if necessary.

3 Rinse the fish fillets under cold running water and pat dry with paper towels.

4 Divide the fish into 4 portions, cutting neatly on the diagonal with the chef's knife. Cut the lemon in half, then cut each lemon half into even-sized wedges. Set aside for decoration.

TARTARE SAUCE

This classic accompaniment adds piquancy to the richness of deep-fried fish. Here the ingredients are roughly chopped, then bound together with creamy mayonnaise. The sauce can be made up to 2 days ahead and kept, covered, in the refrigerator.

 SERVES 4

WORK TIME 20–25 MINUTES

SHOPPING LIST

1	hard-boiled egg
2	gherkin pickles
1 tsp	drained capers
1	small shallot
2–3	sprigs of parsley
2–3	sprigs of fresh chervil or tarragon
1/2 cup	bottled mayonnaise
	salt and pepper

1 Tap the egg to crack the shell. Peel it and rinse with cold water. Coarsely chop the egg.

Coarsely chop ingredients for tartare sauce to add texture

Pickles give sauce refreshing tang

2 With a chef's knife, coarsely chop the gherkin pickles, then the capers.

3 Peel and halve the shallot; set it flat-side down on a chopping board. Slice horizontally toward the root, leaving the slices attached at the root. Slice vertically, again leaving the root end uncut, and cut across the shallot to make fine dice.

4 Strip the parsley leaves and chervil or tarragon leaves from the stems and pile them on the chopping board. Using a chef's knife, hold the tip of the blade against the board and rock the blade back and forth to coarsely chop the herb leaves.

Fold lightly so ingredients are not crushed

5 Mix together the mayonnaise, chopped egg, capers, gherkin pickles, shallot, and herbs and taste for seasoning. Cover and refrigerate until serving.

3 COAT AND DEEP-FRY THE FISH; BROWN THE CHIPS

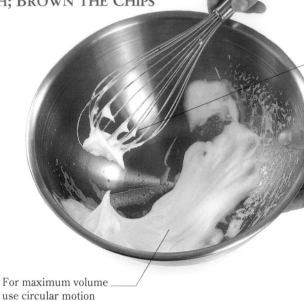

Whites gather in whisk wires when stiff

1 Heat the oven to low. Heat the oil to 375° F. Put the flour on a plate and season with salt and pepper. Coat the pieces of fish with the seasoned flour, patting with your hands so they are evenly coated.

For maximum volume use circular motion when whisking

2 Beat the egg white in a medium metal bowl until stiff peaks form when the whisk is lifted.

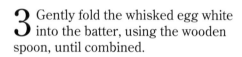

3 Gently fold the whisked egg white into the batter, using the wooden spoon, until combined.

4 Using the 2-pronged fork, dip a piece of fish in the batter, turning to coat thoroughly. Lift it out and hold it over the bowl 5 seconds so excess batter can drip off.

5 Carefully lower the piece of fish into the hot oil and deep-fry, turning once, until golden brown and crisp, 6–8 minutes depending on the thickness of the fish. Coat and deep-fry the remaining fish, 1 or 2 pieces at a time.

ANNE SAYS
"Remove any scraps of batter from the oil in between batches."

Using 2-pronged fork, lower piece of fish gently into hot oil so oil does not bubble up too much

6 As the fish is deep-fried, transfer to the baking sheet lined with paper towels so that excess oil is absorbed. Keep warm in the oven.

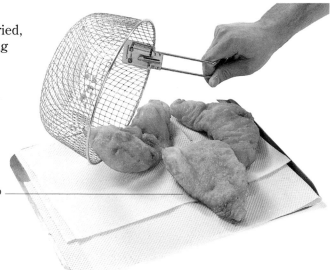

Paper towels absorb excess fat so batter-fried fish remain crisp

7 Put the partially cooked chips in the frying basket and deep-fry until very hot and golden brown, 1–2 minutes. Drain on paper towels.

🍴 **TO SERVE**

Divide the fish and chips among individual warmed plates. Sprinkle the chips with a little salt. Decorate the fish with the lemon wedges and serve at once, accompanied by tartare sauce, if you like.

Chips remain crisp if salt is not sprinkled on until just before serving

VARIATION

TEMPURA-STYLE FISH WITH SWEET POTATOES

A light tempura batter coats this fish, which is served with a Japanese-style dipping sauce.

1 Make the dipping sauce: finely grate about 2 oz daikon or white radish. With a small knife, peel the skin from a 1-inch piece of fresh ginger root. Slice the ginger, cutting across the fibrous grain, then crush each slice with the flat of a chef's knife and finely chop the slices. Mix 1/2 cup sake (rice wine) and 1/2 cup light soy sauce together, then add the grated daikon or radish, chopped ginger, and 1 tsp sugar, or more to taste. Set aside.

2 Make the batter: sift 2 cups flour. Lightly beat 2 eggs in a large shallow bowl. Stir 2 cups cold water into the eggs. Add the flour all at once and mix just until combined; the consistency should be lumpy.

3 Heat the vegetable oil to 375°F. Peel 2 medium sweet potatoes (about 3/4 lb total weight), halve lengthwise, and cut into 1/4-inch slices; it is not necessary to soak them.

4 Coat the sweet potatoes in seasoned flour, then in the batter, and deep-fry until tender and golden, 4–6 minutes; drain and keep warm in a low oven.

5 Rinse and pat dry the fish, then divide into 4 portions, as directed. Coat the fish in the seasoned flour and batter and deep-fry as directed.

6 Serve the fish with the sweet potatoes and dipping sauce. Decorate with fresh chive stems, omitting the lemon wedges.

ENGLISH FISH PIE

🍽 SERVES 6   🍲 WORK TIME 35–45 MINUTES   ♨ BAKING TIME 20–30 MINUTES

EQUIPMENT

2-quart oval pie dish †

whisk

pastry bag and large star tube

vegetable peeler

slotted spoon

strainer

pastry brush

bowls

chef's knife

small knife

large metal spoon

wooden spoon

potato masher

ladle

sauté pan with lid

chopping board

saucepans, 1 with lid

† deep baking dish can also be used

This English favorite uses cooked, flaked white fish, such as haddock, with hard-boiled eggs and shrimp in a fish-flavored white sauce. The pie is then topped with mashed potatoes and browned in the oven for a hearty hot meal.

GETTING AHEAD
The fish pie can be made 1 day ahead, and kept, covered, in the refrigerator. Bake it just before serving.

SHOPPING LIST

3	eggs
1	small onion
1 quart	milk
10	peppercorns
2	bay leaves
1½ lb	skinned haddock fillets
5–7	sprigs of parsley
6 tbsp	butter, more for dish
½ cup	flour
¼ lb	cooked, peeled medium shrimp
	salt and pepper
For the mashed potato topping	
4	medium potatoes, total weight about 1¼ lb
¼ cup	milk
¼ cup	butter

INGREDIENTS

haddock fillets †

shrimp

parsley

potatoes

eggs

milk

flour

peppercorns

bay leaves

onion

butter

† other suitable fish
catfish, cod, grouper, halibut, orange roughy, snapper

ORDER OF WORK

1 **MAKE THE POTATO TOPPING AND HARD-BOIL THE EGGS**

2 **COOK THE FISH AND MAKE THE SAUCE**

3 **ASSEMBLE AND BAKE THE FISH PIE**

1 MAKE THE POTATO TOPPING AND HARD-BOIL THE EGGS

1 Wash and peel the potatoes. Cut them into pieces. Half-fill a medium saucepan with water, add salt, then the potatoes, and bring to a boil.

2 Simmer the potatoes until tender when pierced with the tip of the small knife, 15–20 minutes. Meanwhile, hard-boil and shell the eggs (see box, page 48).

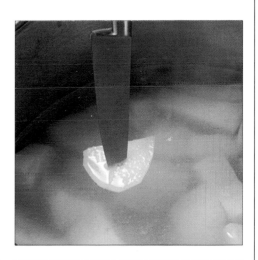

Thoroughly cooked potatoes mash easily

3 Drain the potatoes thoroughly. Using the potato masher, mash the potatoes in the saucepan.

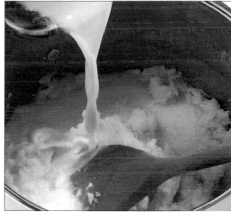

4 Heat the milk in a small saucepan. Add the butter, salt, and pepper to the milk and stir until mixed. Pour the hot milk mixture into the potatoes.

5 Beat the mixture constantly over medium heat until the potatoes are light and fluffy, about 5 minutes. Taste the potatoes for seasoning.

Fold pastry bag over hand for support while filling with mashed potato

6 Let the potatoes cool slightly, then spoon them into the pastry bag fitted with the star tube. Set aside.

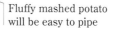

Fluffy mashed potato will be easy to pipe

HOW TO HARD-BOIL AND SHELL EGGS

1 Put the eggs in a medium saucepan of cold water. Bring the water to a boil and simmer the eggs, 10 minutes.

2 Remove the pan from the heat and immediately run cold water into the pan to stop the eggs cooking. Allow the eggs to cool in the water.

3 Drain the eggs. Tap gently to crack the shells all over, then remove the shells. Rinse the eggs and dry with paper towels.

2 COOK THE FISH AND MAKE THE SAUCE

1 Peel and quarter the onion. Pour the milk into the sauté pan, then add the peppercorns, bay leaves, and onion quarters to the milk.

2 Bring the milk mixture to a boil, then remove from the heat. Cover the sauté pan and let stand in a warm place to infuse, about 10 minutes.

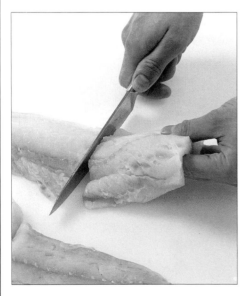

Milk infused with flavorings makes aromatic cooking liquid for fish

4 Add the fish to the milk mixture, cover the pan, and simmer until the fish flakes easily when tested with a fork, 5–10 minutes, depending on the thickness of the fillets.

Fish pieces will cook quickly

3 With the chef's knife, cut each of the fillets across into pieces.

5 Transfer the fish to a large plate, using the slotted spoon; reserve the cooking liquid. Let the fish cool, then flake with a fork.

ANNE SAYS
"To find any leftover bones, pick over the fish with your fingers."

6 Strip the parsley leaves from the stems and pile them on the chopping board. With the chef's knife, coarsely chop the parsley leaves.

Parsley will add fresh flavor to sauce

Pinch off leaves from stems with fingers

7 To make the sauce, gently melt the butter in a medium saucepan over medium heat. Whisk in the flour and cook until foaming, 30–60 seconds.

8 Remove the butter and flour mixture from the heat. Pour the reserved fish cooking liquid through the strainer into the butter and flour mixture.

9 Whisk the liquid into the sauce, then return to the heat, and cook, whisking constantly, until the sauce boils and thickens. Season with salt and pepper and simmer 2 minutes.

! TAKE CARE !
If the sauce forms lumps at any stage, stop heating and whisk vigorously. If this is not sufficient, strain the sauce.

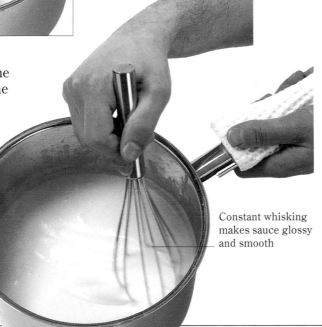

Constant whisking makes sauce glossy and smooth

10 Stir the chopped parsley into the sauce, using the whisk. Taste for seasoning.

3 ASSEMBLE AND BAKE THE FISH PIE

1 Heat the oven to 350° F. Melt some butter and, using the pastry brush, butter the pie dish.

2 Set the hard-boiled eggs on the chopping board and chop them coarsely with the chef's knife.

Grip egg with fingertips as you chop

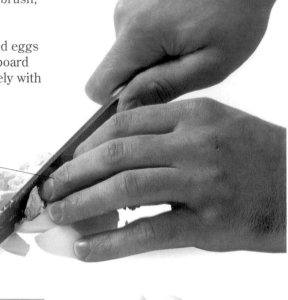

Hard-boiled eggs add body and texture to fish pie

3 Ladle one-third of the sauce into the bottom of the pie dish.

4 Spoon the flaked haddock on top of the sauce, distributing the fish in an even layer.

5 Cover the fish with the remaining sauce, then distribute the shrimp evenly on the surface.

Arrange shrimp on sauce

6 Sprinkle the chopped hard-boiled eggs over the top of the shrimp.

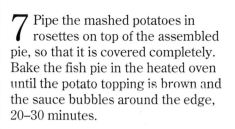

7 Pipe the mashed potatoes in rosettes on top of the assembled pie, so that it is covered completely. Bake the fish pie in the heated oven until the potato topping is brown and the sauce bubbles around the edge, 20–30 minutes.

ANNE SAYS
"Alternatively, spread the potatoes over the top of the fish pie, making peaks with a fork."

Be sure eggs and shrimp are completely covered with potato rosettes

V A R I A T I O N
INDIVIDUAL FISH CRUMBLES
Oat crumble topping isn't just for desserts! This recipe combines rolled oats with parsley and Parmesan cheese to top this English favorite.

1 Follow the main recipe, replacing the potato topping with crumble topping: sift $1^1/_4$ cups flour into a medium bowl. Using 2 table knives, cut 6 tbsp butter into small pieces in the flour.
2 With your fingertips, rub the pieces of butter into the flour until the mixture resembles fine crumbs. Alternatively, blend the butter with the flour in a food processor.
3 Chop the leaves from 3–5 additional sprigs of parsley.
4 Stir $^1/_2$ cup rolled oats, the additional chopped parsley, 1 tbsp grated Parmesan cheese, salt, and pepper into the blended butter and flour.
5 Butter 6 individual casserole dishes and layer the ingredients as directed in the main recipe, dividing them equally among the casserole dishes.
6 Sprinkle the oat crumble topping over the pie filling in each dish, and bake 20–25 minutes.
7 If necessary, brown the individual fish crumbles under the broiler, 1–2 minutes.

🍴 **TO SERVE**
Serve the fish pie hot from the pie dish, onto warmed individual plates.

Piped potato rosettes are an appealing topping

Pie filling is saucy and tasty with a delicious combination of fish and shrimp

SALTIMBOCCA OF SALMON

EQUIPMENT

shallow non-metallic dish

metal spatula

chef's knife

filleting knife

small knife

large frying pan

slotted spoon

paper towels

saucepan

tweezers

wooden toothpicks

bowls

metal skewer

plastic wrap

chopping board

Chef Chambrette, a legend at La Varenne cooking school, introduced me to this variation on traditional saltimbocca of veal. Salmon "scaloppine" are marinated in olive oil and herbs, wrapped around smoked salmon, and sautéed. A light tomato-basil garnish is the finishing touch.

GETTING AHEAD
The salmon slices can be marinated and then rolled up to 4 hours ahead and kept refrigerated. They should be sautéed just before cooking.

plus 1½–2 hours marinating time

INGREDIENTS

fresh salmon fillet †

sliced smoked salmon   olive oil

fresh basil

lemon juice

sugar

bay leaves

tomatoes

butter

fresh thyme

† other suitable fish
sea bass, striped bass

SHOPPING LIST

2 lb	fresh salmon fillet, with its skin
5–7	sprigs of fresh basil
½ lb	sliced smoked salmon
3 tbsp	butter
	salt and pepper
	For the marinade
	juice of ½ lemon
¾ cup	olive oil
3–4	sprigs of fresh thyme
2	bay leaves
	For the tomato-basil garnish
4	tomatoes, total weight about 1¼ lb
1	small bunch of fresh basil
2 tbsp	olive oil
1	pinch of sugar

ORDER OF WORK

1. **PREPARE AND MARINATE THE SALMON SCALOPPINE**

2. **MAKE THE TOMATO-BASIL GARNISH**

3. **ROLL AND COOK THE SALTIMBOCCA**

1 PREPARE AND MARINATE THE SALMON SCALOPPINE

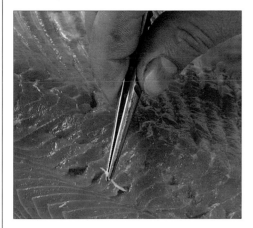

Angle knife slightly to slice very thinly

1 Rinse the salmon fillet with cold water and pat dry with paper towels. If necessary, cut out the remnants of the central bone and pull out any pin bones with the tweezers.

2 With the tail facing away from you and working toward it, use the filleting knife to cut 12 diagonal slices from the salmon, making scaloppine which are as thin and even as possible. Leave any skin behind.

3 Make the marinade: put the lemon juice and oil in the shallow dish. Strip the thyme leaves from the stems and add to the dish with pepper. Crush the bay leaves into the dish.

4 Add the salmon scaloppine to the marinade. Cover and marinate 1 hour in the refrigerator. Meanwhile make the tomato-basil garnish.

2 MAKE THE TOMATO-BASIL GARNISH

Chop basil coarsely to give garnish texture

1 Cut the cores from the tomatoes; score an "x" on the base of each. Immerse in boiling water until the skin starts to split, 8–15 seconds. Transfer to cold water. When cold, peel off the skin. Cut crosswise in half, squeeze out the seeds, then chop.

2 Strip the basil leaves from the stems and pile them on the chopping board. With the chef's knife, coarsely chop the leaves.

3 Mix the tomatoes with the oil and chopped basil and season to taste with salt, pepper, and a pinch of sugar. Let stand to marinate 30–60 minutes at room temperature.

3 ROLL AND COOK THE SALTIMBOCCA

1 Transfer the salmon scaloppine from the marinade to paper towels. Pat dry with paper towels.

2 Strip the basil leaves from the stems. Cut the smoked salmon slices into pieces the same size as the salmon scaloppine.

Fresh basil gives pungent flavor

Fresh and smoked salmon will make tasty contrast

3 Assemble the saltimbocca: arrange a piece of smoked salmon on top of each of 3 salmon scaloppine. Put a basil leaf in the center of each piece of smoked salmon.

4 Roll up the assembled saltimbocca. Secure each with a toothpick, threading it in and out along the seam.

5 Assemble and roll the remaining salmon scaloppine, pieces of smoked salmon, and basil leaves in the same way.

6 Heat the butter in the frying pan and add a batch of salmon saltimbocca, leaving space around them in the pan.

7 Cook the saltimbocca over high heat, turning them occasionally, until lightly browned on all sides, 1–2 minutes.

! TAKE CARE !
Do not overcook the saltimbocca or they will be dry.

Turn to brown lightly and evenly

8 Test the saltimbocca for tenderness by piercing with a skewer. Remove from the pan and keep warm while you cook the remaining saltimbocca.

🍴 TO SERVE
Remove the toothpicks from the saltimbocca. Arrange them on warmed individual plates and serve at once with the tomato-basil garnish.

Fresh spinach pasta ribbons arc a colorful accompaniment to salmon rolls

Tomato-basil garnish is a refreshing complement

PAUPIETTES OF SOLE
Lemon sole fillets take the place of salmon scaloppine in this steamed version of saltimbocca.

1 Make the tomato-basil garnish as directed in the main recipe.
2 Replace the salmon fillet with 6 large skinless fillets of lemon sole (total weight about 1 lb). Trim the fillets and slice each in half along the central line. Flatten the fish gently with the side of a chef's knife. Omit the marinade.
3 Cut the slices of smoked salmon to fit the sole pieces.
4 Lay one piece of sole on the work surface, skinned-side up, and put a piece of smoked salmon on top; omit the basil leaf. Starting from the tail end, roll up fairly tightly. (If the roll is very fat, unroll and cut it crosswise in half to make 2 smaller rolls.) Secure the roll with a wooden toothpick. Continue making the rest of the rolls.
5 Fill a steamer with 2–3 inches of water. Bring the water to a boil. Arrange the rolls on the steamer rack, seam-side down, and sprinkle them with the juice of 1/2 lemon, salt, and pepper. Set the rack over the simmering water, cover, and cook until tender when pierced with a skewer, 8–10 minutes.
6 Slice and serve with the tomato-basil garnish, decorated with fresh basil.

ROAST MONKFISH WITH GARLIC AND CHILI SAUCES

🍽 SERVES 6 🥣 WORK TIME 25–30 MINUTES* ♨ ROASTING TIME 12–15 MINUTES

EQUIPMENT

shallow glass dish

small saucepan

small knife

pastry brush

chef's knife

food processor

whisk

rubber spatula

bowls

paper towels

chopping board

baking sheet

aluminum foil

rubber gloves

Monkfish, also called anglerfish, is ugly, with a huge head and gaping mouth, but its excellent flesh more than compensates for its disconcerting appearance. These monkfish fillets are roasted whole, then sliced to serve hot or at room temperature with two pungent sauces.

*plus 2 hours marinating time

SHOPPING LIST

6	skinned monkfish fillets, total weight 3 lb
5–7	sprigs of fresh oregano
5–7	sprigs of fresh thyme
2 tbsp	olive oil
	salt and pepper
	For the garlic and chili sauces
4	eggs
3 tbsp	butter
3 tbsp	flour
1 cup	boiling water
8	garlic cloves, or to taste
½ cup	olive oil
6–9	sprigs of parsley and other fresh herbs such as thyme, oregano, chervil, and tarragon
2	fresh hot red chili peppers
2 tsp	tomato paste
	cayenne (optional)

INGREDIENTS

monkfish fillets†

hot red chili peppers

tomato paste

fresh thyme

butter

flour

parsley

olive oil

eggs

cayenne (optional)

fresh oregano

garlic cloves

† other suitable fish
bluefish, sea bass

ORDER OF WORK

1 PREPARE AND MARINATE THE MONKFISH

2 MAKE THE SAUCES AND DECORATION

3 ROAST THE MONKFISH

PREPARE AND MARINATE THE MONKFISH

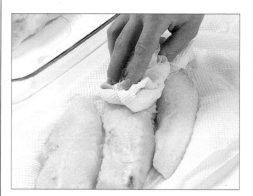

1 If necessary, cut away the thin membrane that covers the flesh of the monkfish fillets. Rinse the fillets with cold water, then transfer to paper towels and pat dry.

2 Strip the oregano and thyme leaves from the stems and pile them on the chopping board. Roughly chop the leaves.

3 Put the fillets in the shallow dish and sprinkle with the olive oil, chopped herbs, salt, and pepper. Toss with your hands so the fillets are covered with oil. Cover and marinate in the refrigerator for 2 hours. Meanwhile, make the sauces.

Lift and turn fillets with your hands

Herb marinade adds flavor to monkfish fillets

MAKE THE SAUCES AND DECORATION

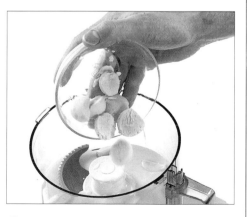

1 Put the eggs in the saucepan, cover with cold water, and bring to a boil. Simmer 10 minutes. Drain the eggs, then let cool in a bowl of cold water. Tap the eggs to crack the shells, then peel them. Separate the yolks from the whites and discard the whites or set them aside for another use.

2 Melt the butter in the saucepan. Whisk in the flour and cook until foaming, about 1 minute. Take from the heat and whisk in the boiling water. The sauce will thicken at once. Return the saucepan to the heat and cook, whisking, 1 minute.

3 Transfer the sauce to the food processor. Peel the garlic cloves. Add to the processor with the hard-boiled egg yolks, salt, and pepper and purée until smooth.

ANNE SAYS
"Add more or less garlic to your taste."

4 With the blades turning, pour in the olive oil in a thin stream, so the sauce thickens and becomes creamy. Taste the sauce for seasoning. Put half of the sauce in a bowl and reserve for the chili sauce.

! TAKE CARE !
If the oil is added too quickly, the mixture will separate.

5 Strip the parsley and other herb leaves from the stems and add to the remaining sauce in the processor. Purée briefly. Transfer to a second bowl. Cover and chill in the refrigerator until serving.

HOW TO CORE, SEED, AND CHOP HOT CHILI PEPPERS

Be sure to wear rubber gloves and avoid contact with eyes; hot chili peppers can burn hands and eyes.

1 Cut the peppers lengthwise in half with a small knife. Cut out the core and fleshy white ribs.

Sauce added to red chili pepper and tomato paste will have vivid color

6 Rinse out the food processor. Core, seed, and chop 1 of the hot chili peppers (see box, left). Put in the processor. Add the tomato paste and the reserved sauce.

2 Scrape out the seeds with the point of a small knife, then roughly chop the pepper halves.

7 Purée until smooth, scraping the sauce from the side of the food processor with the rubber spatula. Season with cayenne, if desired. Transfer to a bowl, cover, and chill.

8 Cut out the core from the second chili pepper and remove the seeds with the tip of the small knife. Cut the chili pepper into thin rings and reserve for the decoration.

3 ROAST THE MONKFISH

1 Heat the oven to 450°F. Line the baking sheet with foil. Arrange the monkfish fillets, side by side, on the foil. Spoon the marinade from the dish over the fillets.

Brush makes basting easy during roasting

2 Roast the fillets in the heated oven, brushing occasionally with the juices which have collected on the foil, until browned and the fish is no longer rare in the center, 12–15 minutes. The flesh should just flake when tested with a fork.

🍽 TO SERVE
Cut the monkfish into diagonal slices. Arrange on individual warmed plates, add a little of each sauce, and decorate with the chili rings. Serve the remaining sauces separately.

Piquant chili sauce contrasts with sweet flavor of monkfish

VARIATION

BROILED MONKFISH SCALOPPINE WITH GARLIC AND CHILI SAUCES

Monkfish fillets are cut into thin slices, broiled, and served with these colorful sauces.

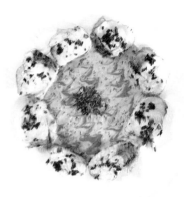

1 Rinse and pat dry the monkfish fillets. Holding each fillet steady with your hand, cut diagonal slices about ³⁄₈ inch thick, working toward the tail and keeping the slices of monkfish as even as possible.
2 Marinate the monkfish slices as directed, using twice the amount of chopped herbs. Meanwhile, make the garlic and chili sauces as directed. Omit the chili pepper rings.
3 Broil the monkfish scaloppine about 3 inches from the heat for 4 minutes; it is not necessary to turn them.
4 Make pools of garlic sauce on warmed individual plates. Drizzle lines of chili sauce onto each and draw a knife across at even intervals to create a feathered effect. Arrange the fish around the edge of each plate. Decorate with fresh herbs.

Monkfish slices well for presentation

— GETTING AHEAD —
The garlic and chili sauces can be made up to 1 day ahead and kept refrigerated. Roast the monkfish just before serving.

SEAFOOD LASAGNE

 SERVES 8   WORK TIME 40–45 MINUTES   BAKING TIME 30–45 MINUTES

EQUIPMENT

9- x 13-inch baking dish

saucepans, 1 with lid

chef's knife

whisk

chopping board

ladle

slotted spoon

paper towels

small knife

wooden spoon

cheese grater

strainer

wide shallow pan

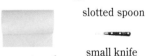
bowls

colander

This partnership of pasta with seafood, layered with a rich sauce, is delicious. The seafood is first lightly sautéed with shallots and white wine, then the cooking liquid is added to the sauce.

SHOPPING LIST

½ lb	medium raw shrimp
½ lb	sea or bay scallops
1 lb	sole fillets
2	shallots
2 tbsp	butter, more for baking dish
¼ cup	white wine
1 tbsp	vegetable oil
½ lb	fresh or dried lasagne noodles
3 oz	Gruyère cheese
	salt and pepper
For the sauce	
1	small onion
2 cups	milk
1	bay leaf
6	peppercorns
1 lb	plum tomatoes
6 oz	mushrooms
2 tbsp	butter
¼ cup	flour
⅔ cup	heavy cream
6–8	sprigs of fresh parsley and basil
¼ tsp	hot red pepper flakes, more to taste

INGREDIENTS

sole fillets†

medium raw shrimp

lasagne noodles

scallops

white wine

fresh herbs

heavy cream

bay leaf

shallots

vegetable oil

butter

flour

mushrooms

Gruyère cheese

milk

plum tomatoes

onion

hot red pepper flakes

peppercorns

---

† other suitable fish
catfish, flounder, grouper, mahi mahi, orange roughy

ORDER OF WORK

1 PREPARE THE SEAFOOD

2 MAKE THE SAUCE

3 ASSEMBLE AND BAKE THE LASAGNE

1 PREPARE THE SEAFOOD

Peel shell from shrimp starting at head end, then tail can be nipped off easily

1 Peel off the shells from the shrimp. Make a shallow cut along the back of each shrimp and remove the dark intestinal vein. If the shrimp are large, cut them lengthwise in half.

2 If necessary, remove and discard the tough muscle at the side of each scallop. Rinse the scallops with cold water, drain, and pat them dry with paper towels.

3 Using the small knife, cut large scallops crosswise in half.

Slice across fillets to cut into pieces

Pieces of fish will be easy to distribute evenly in dish

4 Rinse the sole fillets with cold water and pat dry with paper towels. Cut into several pieces. Refrigerate until ready to use.

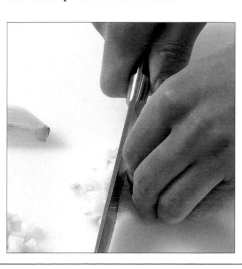

5 Peel the shallots and separate into sections if necessary. Slice horizontally toward the root, leaving the slices attached at the root. Slice vertically, again leaving the root end uncut, then cut across the shallot to make fine dice.

6 Heat the butter in a medium saucepan. Add the chopped shallots and sauté, stirring, until soft but not brown, 1–2 minutes. Add the shrimp and scallops, and season with salt and pepper.

Do not overcook
shrimp or they
will be tough

Cooking liquid
will enrich sauce

7 Cook over medium heat until the shrimp turn pink and the scallops become opaque, 2–3 minutes. Add the white wine and bring just to a boil.

8 Remove the pan from the heat. With the slotted spoon, lift out the shrimp and scallops and reserve them. Set the cooking liquid aside.

2 MAKE THE SAUCE

1 Peel and quarter the onion. In a saucepan, combine the onion, bay leaf, milk, and peppercorns. Bring to a boil, then cover and keep in a warm place, 10 minutes. Meanwhile, peel, seed, and chop the tomatoes (see box, page 64).

ANNE SAYS
"To save time, you can use 1 cup drained canned plum tomatoes."

Infusing milk
with onion adds
extra flavor

Flavored milk will
make aromatic
addition to sauce

2 Wipe the mushroom caps with damp paper towels and trim the stems even with the caps. Set the mushrooms stem-side down on the chopping board and slice them.

3 Add the sliced mushrooms to the reserved shrimp and scallop cooking liquid and simmer 2 minutes. Set aside.

4 Melt the butter in another saucepan over medium heat. Whisk in the flour and cook until foaming, 30–60 seconds.

Straining removes flavorings

5 Take the pan from the heat; let cool slightly, then strain in the milk. Whisk to mix. Return to the heat and cook, whisking constantly, until the sauce boils and thickens, 2–3 minutes. Season with salt and pepper and simmer about 2 minutes. Remove from heat.

6 Pour the heavy cream into the white sauce and then whisk vigorously to mix.

! TAKE CARE !
If the sauce forms lumps at any stage, whisk vigorously off the heat. If whisking is not sufficient, strain the sauce.

7 Add the mushrooms with their cooking liquid to the saucepan, then add the chopped tomatoes. Return the pan to the heat and simmer 2 minutes.

Tomatoes and mushrooms give sauce its character

8 Strip the parsley and basil leaves from the stems and coarsely chop.

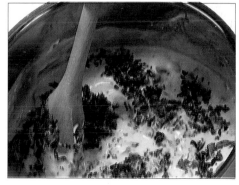

9 Stir the herbs into the sauce with the red pepper flakes, salt, and pepper. Set the sauce aside.

HOW TO PEEL, SEED, AND CHOP TOMATOES

Tomatoes are often peeled and seeded before chopping so they will cook to form a smooth purée.

1 Bring a small pan of water to a boil. Using a small knife, cut out the cores from the tomatoes. Score an "x" on the base of each tomato. Immerse the tomatoes in the water and boil until the skin starts to split, 8–15 seconds. Using a slotted spoon, transfer them at once to a bowl of cold water to stop cooking.

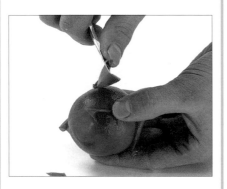

2 When cold, peel the skin from the tomatoes with a small knife. Cut them crosswise in half and squeeze out the seeds.

3 Set each tomato half cut-side down and slice it. Give it a half turn and slice again. Chop the flesh coarsely or finely, as required.

3 ASSEMBLE AND BAKE THE LASAGNE

1 Fill the wide shallow pan with water, bring to a boil, and add the oil and 1 tbsp salt. Add the lasagne noodles one by one and simmer until barely tender, 3–5 minutes for fresh lasagne, 8–10 minutes for dried, or according to package directions.

2 Using the slotted spoon, lift out the lasagne noodles and put them into the colander. Rinse with cold water and drain again thoroughly. When cold, spread out on a clean dish towel to dry. Grate the Gruyère cheese.

3 Heat the oven to 350° F. Butter the baking dish. Ladle one-quarter of the sauce over the bottom of the prepared dish and arrange half of the shrimp and scallops on top.

Dot the sauce with shrimp and scallops

4 Cover the sauce and shrimp and scallop mixture with a layer of lasagne noodles.

5 Put the fish pieces in one layer on top of the lasagne. Coat the fish with one-third of the remaining sauce and cover with lasagne noodles.

6 Add the rest of the shrimp and scallops followed by half of the remaining sauce, then cover with the remaining lasagne noodles. Ladle the remaining sauce evenly over the top. Sprinkle with the grated Gruyère cheese.

Final sprinkling of cheese ensures browned topping

Creamy sauce tops seafood

7 Bake the lasagne in the heated oven until bubbling and golden brown on top, 30–45 minutes.

🍽 **TO SERVE**
Cut the lasagne into squares and serve hot from the baking dish onto warmed individual plates.

Crispy topping gives crunch and texture

V A R I A T I O N

SMOKED TROUT AND SPINACH LASAGNE

In this colorful lasagne, smoked trout and shrimp are arranged between layers of spinach lasagne noodles.

1 Prepare and cook 1 lb large raw shrimp as directed; omit the scallops.
2 Replace the sole fillets with the same quantity of smoked trout. Cut the trout into large pieces.
3 Make the sauce as directed.
4 Use spinach lasagne noodles in place of plain lasagne noodles.
5 Assemble and bake the lasagne as directed in the main recipe.
6 Serve decorated with salad and herb leaves, if you like.

— **GETTING AHEAD** —
The seafood and sauce can be prepared, and the lasagne assembled up to 1 day ahead and kept, covered, in the refrigerator. Bake the lasagne just before serving.

STEAMED BRAIDED FISH WITH WARM VINAIGRETTE

🍽 SERVES 6　　🥣 WORK TIME 35–40 MINUTES　　🍲 COOKING TIME 8–10 MINUTES

EQUIPMENT

steamer†

chopping board

saucepan

chef's knife

small knife

slotted spatula

whisk

paper towels

† large pot with lid and rack can also be used

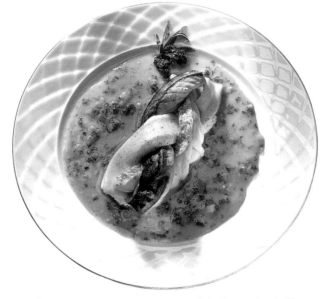

In this recipe, 3 varieties of fish with different colored skins are cut into strips, braided, then steamed over a court bouillon, an aromatic cooking liquid. The braids are served with a warm herb-dotted vinaigrette.

SHOPPING LIST

³/₄ lb	snapper fillets, with their skin
³/₄ lb	sole fillets, with their skin
³/₄ lb	mackerel fillets, with their skin
	salt and pepper
For the court bouillon	
1	carrot
1	onion
1 quart	water
1	bouquet garni made with 5–6 parsley stems, 2–3 sprigs of fresh thyme, and 1 bay leaf
6	peppercorns
2	whole cloves
For the warm vinaigrette	
2	shallots
¹/₂ cup	red wine vinegar
2 tsp	Dijon-style mustard
¹/₃ cup	olive oil
²/₃ cup	vegetable oil
5–7	sprigs of fresh tarragon or thyme
7–10	sprigs of fresh parsley or chervil

INGREDIENTS

sole fillets†

mackerel fillets†

snapper fillets†

parsley

shallots

onion

bouquet garni

olive oil　vegetable oil

carrot

Dijon-style mustard

fresh tarragon

peppercorns

red wine vinegar

cloves

† other suitable fish
any fish with thin, colorful skin such as drum, jack, red mullet, sea or striped bass

ORDER OF WORK

1 PREPARE COURT BOUILLON AND FISH

2 STEAM THE BRAIDED FISH

3 MAKE THE VINAIGRETTE; FINISH THE DISH

1 PREPARE COURT BOUILLON AND FISH

1 Peel and quarter the carrot and onion. Combine the water, bouquet garni, peppercorns, 1 tsp salt, the cloves, carrot, and onion in the bottom of the steamer and bring just to a boil. There should be about 2 inches of court bouillon in the steamer. Simmer 20–30 minutes.

2 Meanwhile, rinse the fish fillets with cold water; pat dry with paper towels. Discard any bones. Trim the fillets so they are roughly the same length.

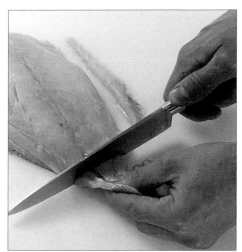

Shimmering snapper contributes to colorful braid

Mackerel skin is beautifully marked

3 Cut the fillets lengthwise into strips about 1/2– 3/4 inch wide, so that you have 6 strips of each fish.

! TAKE CARE !
Handle fish gently while cutting so strips do not break.

Braid strips loosely so they do not shrink and break during cooking

Braids do not have to be even

4 Arrange a strip of snapper, sole, and mackerel next to each other, skin-side up. Braid the strips together, lifting them carefully over each other and gathering the ends together. Continue making braids with the remaining strips of fish.

HOW TO CHOP HERBS

Parsley, tarragon, thyme, chives, rosemary, dill, and basil are herbs that are usually chopped before being added to other ingredients. Do not chop delicate herbs like basil too finely because their leaves bruise easily.

Pull off herb leaves gently to ensure they retain maximum freshness

1 Strip the leaves or sprigs from the stems. Pile the leaves or sprigs on a chopping board.

2 Cut the leaves or sprigs into small pieces, holding the herbs together in a bunch with one hand while chopping with the chef's knife. Holding the tip of the knife blade against the board with your fingertips, and rocking the blade back and forth, continue chopping until the herbs are coarse or fine, as you wish.

2 STEAM THE BRAIDED FISH

1 With the slotted spatula, transfer the braids to the steamer rack. Sprinkle them with salt and pepper.

ANNE SAYS
"You may have to steam the fish braids in 2 batches."

Season braids to taste

Leave space between braids in steamer

2 Set the rack over the simmering court bouillon; there should be 2 inches of liquid. Cover the steamer.

! TAKE CARE !
If too much liquid evaporates from the steamer, add more water.

3 Steam the braids until the fish just flakes easily when tested with a fork, 8–10 minutes. Meanwhile, make the vinaigrette.

3 MAKE THE VINAIGRETTE; FINISH THE DISH

1 Peel each shallot and slice horizontally toward the root, leaving the slices attached at the root. Slice vertically, then cut across the shallot to make fine dice. Strip the herb leaves from the stems, reserving 4 sprigs of each for garnish. Finely chop the leaves (see box, page 68).

🍽 TO SERVE
Spoon the vinaigrette onto 6 individual warmed plates. Transfer the braids to the plates. Garnish with the reserved parsley and tarragon sprigs, and serve at once.

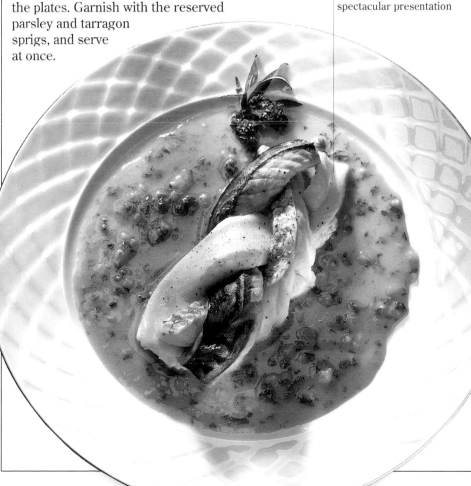

2 In the saucepan, whisk together the vinegar, mustard, and shallots. Add the olive oil, then the vegetable oil in a steady stream, whisking constantly so the vinaigrette emulsifies and thickens slightly. Heat gently until warm, whisking constantly. Remove from the heat and whisk in the herbs and salt and pepper to taste.

Braids of fish make a spectacular presentation

VARIATION

PANACHE OF STEAMED FISH WITH WARM SHERRY VINAIGRETTE

A "panaché," or selection, of fish features here with a warm sherry vinaigrette as accompaniment. Green beans are a good complement.

1 Make the court bouillon as directed.
2 Rinse the fish fillets and pat dry. Cut the fish into even diamond shapes.
3 Steam the fish pieces as for the braids, allowing 5–7 minutes, depending on their thickness. If the steamer is crowded, cook the fish pieces in 2 batches.
4 Meanwhile, prepare the warm vinaigrette as directed in the main recipe, substituting sherry vinegar for the red wine vinegar and walnut oil for the olive oil. Omit the herbs.
5 Arrange the fish on warmed individual plates, skin-side up. Spoon a little of the warm sherry vinaigrette over the fish and serve the remainder separately.

GETTING AHEAD
The vinaigrette can be made up to 1 day ahead. The court bouillon can be made and the fish braided up to 1 hour ahead. Just before serving, warm the vinaigrette and add the herbs while the fish is steaming.

MONKFISH AMERICAINE

 SERVES 4–6   WORK TIME 45–50 MINUTES   COOKING TIME 35–40 MINUTES

EQUIPMENT

saucepans

kitchen scissors

bowl

kitchen string

vegetable peeler

filleting knife

sauté pan †

chef's knife

small ladle

strainer

paper towels

wooden spoon

whisk

metal spatula

chopping board

† large frying pan can also be used

Known as the poor man's lobster for its sweetness and "meaty" texture, monkfish has grown increasingly popular in recent years. Here, it is served with a tomato, garlic, and Cognac sauce.

SHOPPING LIST

3-lb	piece of monkfish, on the bone
2	medium onions
1/2 cup	white wine or juice of 1/2 lemon
1 tsp	peppercorns
3–5	sprigs of parsley
2 cups	water
1/4 cup	flour
	salt and pepper
2 tbsp	olive oil
1/2 cup	butter
	rice pilaf (see box, page 74) for serving (optional)
For the Américaine sauce	
1	carrot
2	garlic cloves
1 1/2 lb	tomatoes
3–4	sprigs of fresh tarragon
1	bouquet garni (see box, page 72)
2/3 cup	white wine
3 tbsp	Cognac
1	pinch of cayenne pepper (optional)
1 tbsp	tomato paste
1/4 cup	heavy cream
1	pinch of sugar (optional)

INGREDIENTS

monkfish †

white wine

parsley sprigs

carrot

onions

olive oil

heavy cream

tomatoes

peppercorns

flour

garlic cloves

tomato paste

Cognac

bouquet garni

butter

fresh tarragon

† other suitable fish
mahi-mahi, shark

ORDER OF WORK

1 PREPARE THE MONKFISH

2 MAKE THE STOCK; PREPARE SAUCE INGREDIENTS

3 COOK THE FISH; MAKE THE SAUCE

1 PREPARE THE MONKFISH

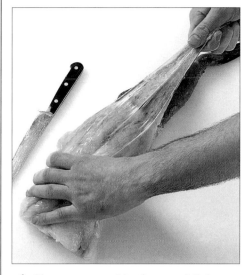

1 If necessary, skin the monkfish: using the filleting knife, cut and release the black skin, then pull it off.

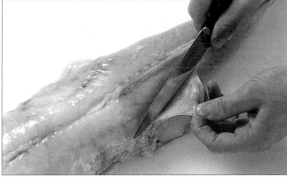

2 Cut away the thin membrane that covers the fish, cutting close to the flesh with the filleting knife, and pulling the membrane away from the fish with your fingers.

ANNE SAYS
"The spine in monkfish has no lateral bones, so once the skin and covering thin white membrane have been removed, the fish can be filleted easily to yield two thick boneless pieces of meat."

3 Cut along one side of the central backbone to remove 1 monkfish fillet. Repeat the process on the other side of the bone to remove the second fillet. Rinse the monkfish fillets with cold water and pat them dry with paper towels.

Ease fillet away from bone with fingertips as you cut

Fillets are easy to remove from central backbone

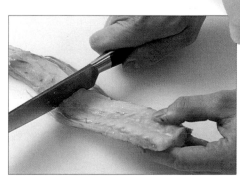

4 With the chef's knife, cut the bone in pieces and reserve the pieces for the fish stock.

Cut slices of uniform thickness

5 Cut each fillet into ½-inch slices. Slightly flatten each slice with the side of the chef's knife.

2 MAKE THE STOCK; PREPARE SAUCE INGREDIENTS

1 Peel and chop the onions. Put half of the chopped onions in a large saucepan and add the monkfish bones, wine, peppercorns, parsley, and water.

2 Bring slowly to a boil, then simmer, uncovered, for 20 minutes. Strain the fish stock into the bowl and let cool.

ANNE SAYS
"You should have about 2 cups of stock."

HOW TO MAKE A BOUQUET GARNI

This package of aromatic flavoring herbs is designed to be easily lifted from the pot and discarded at the end of cooking. To make a bouquet garni, hold 2–3 sprigs of fresh thyme, 1 bay leaf, and 5–6 parsley stems together. Wind a piece of string around the herb stems and tie them together securely, leaving a length of string to tie the bouquet garni to the pan handle.

3 While stock is cooling, peel and trim the carrot. Cut it lengthwise into quarters, then across into 1/2-inch pieces. Set the flat side of the chef's knife on top of each garlic clove and strike it with your fist. Discard the skin and finely chop the garlic.

4 Remove the cores from the tomatoes, then cut each tomato in half. Coarsely chop the halves.

ANNE SAYS
"You will not need to peel and seed the tomatoes because the sauce will be strained."

5 Strip the tarragon leaves from the stems and pile them on the chopping board. Coarsely chop the leaves and reserve for garnish. Set aside the stems for the sauce.

Herbs infuse ingredients with fresh aroma

Wind string around herb stems

Tear leaves gently from stems to avoid bruising

3 COOK THE FISH; MAKE THE SAUCE

1 Put the flour on a plate and season with salt and pepper. Lightly coat the monkfish slices with the seasoned flour, patting with your hands so the slices are evenly coated.

2 Heat the oil and one-quarter of the butter in the sauté pan, add half of the fish slices and sauté, turning once, until brown on both sides, 2–3 minutes. Transfer the slices to a plate with the metal spatula. Sauté the remaining monkfish slices and transfer to the plate.

3 Add the carrot, garlic, and the remaining onion to the sauté pan and cook, stirring to mix in the browned flour from the bottom of the pan, until soft but not brown, 3–5 minutes.

4 Add the tomatoes, white wine, Cognac, tarragon stems, salt and pepper, and a pinch of cayenne, if you like. Tie the bouquet garni to the pan handle. Pour the stock into the pan. Bring to a boil and simmer until slightly thickened, 15–20 minutes.

Bouquet garni tied to handle of pan will be easy to remove before sauce is strained

5 Strain the sauce into a large saucepan, pressing with the ladle to extract all the liquid from the ingredients. Boil until thickened and reduced, 5–10 minutes.

6 Whisk in the heavy cream and tomato paste until the sauce is an even color. Taste the sauce for seasoning, adding a pinch of sugar if it is too acidic.

RICE PILAF

When making pilaf, the rice is first quickly fried in vegetable oil to help keep the grains separate as the rice simmers. It is then cooked in a measured amount of water so the liquid is all absorbed during cooking, leaving the rice light, tender, and flaky.

🍴 SERVES 4–6

🥣 WORK TIME 5–10 MINUTES

♨ COOKING TIME 20 MINUTES

SHOPPING LIST

1	medium onion
2 tbsp	vegetable oil
1½ cups	long-grain rice
3 cups	water
	salt and pepper

1 Peel and chop the onion. Heat the oil in a heavy-based saucepan, add the onion, and cook, stirring, until soft but not brown, 1–2 minutes.

2 Add the rice and cook, stirring, until the oil is absorbed and the rice looks translucent, 2–3 minutes.

Stir rice in oil to keep grains separate

3 Pour the water into the saucepan, season the rice with salt and pepper, and bring to a boil.

4 Cover the pan, reduce the heat, and simmer until all the liquid is absorbed and the rice is tender, about 20 minutes. Let stand, still covered, 10 minutes, then stir with a fork.

7 Add the monkfish slices to the sauce and simmer until just tender, 5–10 minutes.

Monkfish will absorb flavor from sauce

8 Take the saucepan from the heat and add the remaining butter, in small pieces, shaking the saucepan so the butter melts and is mixed into the sauce.

¶◎¶ TO SERVE
Serve the monkfish, sprinkled with the reserved chopped tarragon, on warmed individual plates. Accompany with rice pilaf, if you like.

Monkfish slices are just tender to the bite

SALT COD AMERICAINE

1 Soak 1½ lb salt cod in cold water 1–2 days, changing the water several times. Drain the fish, put it in a large pan of cold water, cover, and bring just to a boil. Simmer until barely tender, about 25 minutes. Drain and let cool slightly. Flake the cod with a fork, discarding any skin and bones.
2 Make the Américaine sauce, using water if you have no fish bones for stock, and omitting the tarragon. Peel and seed the tomatoes before chopping: cut out the cores and score an "x" on the base of each. Immerse in boiling water until the skin starts to split, 8–15 seconds. Transfer at once to cold water. When cold, peel off the skin. Cut crosswise in half and squeeze out the seeds. Finish the sauce as directed but do not strain it. Discard the bouquet garni.
3 While the sauce is simmering, make rice pilaf (see box, page 74).
4 Add the flaked salt cod to the sauce and cook until tender, 5–10 minutes.
5 Pack the hot rice pilaf into 6 buttered ramekins (1 cup capacity). Let stand 2 minutes, then unmold onto warmed individual plates. Spoon the salt cod and sauce beside the rice. Decorate with fresh dill sprigs.

— **GETTING AHEAD** —
The monkfish and sauce can be cooked up to 1 day ahead and kept, covered, in the refrigerator. Reheat on top of the stove, taking care not to overcook the fish.

TURBANS OF SOLE WITH WILD MUSHROOM MOUSSE

 SERVES 4    WORK TIME 20–25 MINUTES*   BAKING TIME 35–45 MINUTES

EQUIPMENT

chef's knife

filleting knife

small knife

food processor†

baking dishes

3-cup soufflé dish

bowls

pastry brush

frying pans

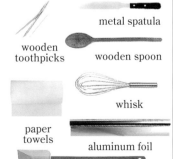

pastry bag with large star tube‡   chopping board

metal spatula

wooden toothpicks   wooden spoon

whisk

paper towels   aluminum foil

rubber spatula

† blender can also be used
‡ plain tube can also be used

INGREDIENTS

sole fillets†

fresh shiitake mushrooms   heavy cream

butter

dry white wine   Madeira

egg

egg yolk

fresh coriander

† other suitable fish
flounder, turbot, whitefish

Sole fillets are shaped into rings, turban-fashion, filled with a wild mushroom mousse, then baked to serve with a fresh coriander and butter sauce. Plain boiled rice would be my choice of accompaniment.

GETTING AHEAD

The mousse can be made up to 1 day ahead and kept refrigerated. Bake the turbans just before serving.

* plus 1 hour chilling time

SHOPPING LIST

6	skinless sole fillets, total weight about 1 lb
½ cup	dry white wine
3–5	sprigs of fresh coriander (cilantro), more for garnish
½ cup	butter, chilled
	For the wild mushroom mousse
5 oz	fresh, or 1 oz dried, shiitake mushrooms
2–3	sprigs of fresh coriander (cilantro)
2 tbsp	butter, more for dishes and foil
	salt and pepper
1	egg
1	egg yolk
1 tbsp	Madeira
½ cup	heavy cream

ORDER OF WORK

1 MAKE THE WILD MUSHROOM MOUSSE

2 PREPARE AND BAKE THE SOLE TURBANS

3 MAKE THE CORIANDER SAUCE

1 MAKE THE WILD MUSHROOM MOUSSE

1 Wipe fresh shiitake mushrooms with damp paper towels and trim the stems, using the small knife. Cut the mushrooms into medium slices. Strip the leaves from the coriander stems and roughly chop.

ANNE SAYS

"If using dried shiitake mushrooms, soak them in a bowl of warm water until plump, about 30 minutes. Drain them and continue as for fresh mushrooms."

Curl fingers to hold mushroom cap securely when slicing

Set mushrooms stem-side down to slice

2 Heat the butter in a medium frying pan. Add the mushrooms with salt and pepper. Cook, stirring constantly, until the liquid has all evaporated, 3–5 minutes. Remove from the heat and let the mixture cool slightly.

Put mixture in bowl for chilling

3 Put the mushrooms in the food processor and purée them. With the blade turning, add the whole egg and the egg yolk. Purée until smooth. Add the Madeira and coriander leaves, and purée just until combined.

4 Mix in salt and pepper, then transfer the puréed mushroom mixture to a bowl. Cover and chill about 1 hour. Fold the cream into the mushroom mixture.

Scrape all mixture from bowl with rubber spatula

5 Heat the oven to 375°F. Brush the inside of the soufflé dish with melted butter.

Mousse mixture will not stick to buttered dish

6 Transfer the chilled mousse mixture from the bowl to the prepared soufflé dish.

Pour hot water carefully around soufflé dish so that liquid does not splash into mousse

Be sure hot water comes well up side of dish so heat is diffused

7 Set the soufflé dish in a baking dish and add enough hot water to come halfway up the side of the soufflé dish.

8 Transfer the baking dish to the heated oven and bake just until set when lightly pressed with your finger, 20–25 minutes. Remove the mousse from the baking dish and let cool while preparing the sole turbans. Reduce the oven temperature to 350°F.

2 PREPARE AND BAKE THE SOLE TURBANS

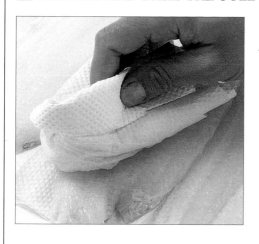

1 Rinse the sole fillets with cold water. Transfer them to paper towels and carefully pat the fillets dry.

2 With the filleting knife, cut each of the sole fillets lengthwise in half.

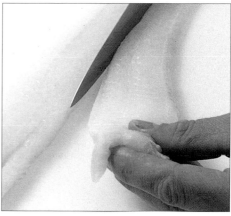

Wooden toothpicks hold circles of sole in place

3 Shape each fillet half into a 3-inch ring, skinned-side in, with the tail end around the outside. Secure with toothpicks. Using a shallow baking dish that will hold all the rings comfortably, brush the dish with melted butter, then arrange the sole in the dish.

4 Fold the top of the pastry bag, fitted with the large star tube, over your hand to form a collar. Spoon in the wild mushroom mousse.

5 Twist the top of the bag, then pipe the mousse in a swirl into the center of each sole ring so that each of the rings is completely filled.

6 Carefully pour the white wine around the sole turbans in the baking dish.

Stuffed turbans cooked in white wine will keep moist in oven

7 Butter a piece of foil and use to cover the sole turbans in the baking dish.

Cooking liquid is essential to sauce

8 Bake in the heated oven until the fish is white and opaque, and the mousse is firm to the touch, 15–20 minutes.

9 Transfer the turbans to a warmed serving plate and reserve the cooking liquid. Remove the toothpicks from the turbans. Keep warm while making the sauce.

3 MAKE THE CORIANDER SAUCE

1 Strip the leaves from the coriander stems, then pile the leaves on the chopping board. With the chef's knife, finely chop the leaves.

2 Cut the chilled butter into small even-sized pieces using the small knife.

3 Pour the cooking liquid from the baking dish into a small frying pan. Boil until reduced to about 2 tbsp.

Add butter
pieces gradually

4 Take from the heat and add the butter, a little at a time, whisking constantly and moving the pan on and off the heat. The sauce should thicken to a creamy consistency.

Coriander sauce adds color and richness to stuffed sole turbans

5 Whisk in the chopped coriander. Taste the sauce for seasoning.

🍽️ **TO SERVE**

Pour the coriander sauce over and around the sole turbans. Garnish each turban with a fresh coriander leaf.

V A R I A T I O N
TURBANS OF FLOUNDER WITH SPINACH MOUSSE

Green spinach mousse makes a pretty filling for turbans of flounder, served here with a tomato-flavored butter sauce.

1 Discard the stems from 1¹/₂ lb fresh spinach; wash the leaves thoroughly. Bring a large pan of water to a boil, add salt, then the spinach, and blanch 1 minute. Drain in a colander, rinse with cold water, and squeeze in your fists to remove all water.

2 Make the mousse as directed, substituting spinach for the shiitake mushrooms and omitting the Madeira. Add a pinch of ground coriander with the salt and pepper.

3 Substitute 6 flounder fillets, weighing about 1 lb, for the sole, and prepare and shape into rings as directed in the main recipe.

4 Fill the flounder rings with the cooked spinach mousse and bake as directed.

5 Make the sauce, omitting the fresh coriander. Whisk in 1 tbsp tomato paste after all the butter has been added.

6 Serve the turbans on warmed individual plates with the sauce spooned around them. Sautéed sliced new potatoes are an ideal accompaniment.

Two-Color Fish Terrine with Citrus-Ginger Sauce

🍽 SERVES 8   🥣 WORK TIME 30–35 MINUTES   🍲 BAKING TIME 1¼–1½ HOURS

EQUIPMENT

12- x 3½- x 3-inch terrine mold with lid

slotted spoon   small knife †

metal skewer

rubber spatula

saucepans

strainer

whisk

vegetable peeler

citrus juicer

wooden spoon

food processor   chef's knife

filleting knife

pastry brush

roasting pan   bowls

paper towels

† tweezers can also be used

INGREDIENTS

fresh salmon fillet †

sole fillets   smoked salmon

fresh ginger root   lemon

lime   parsley sprigs

egg whites   unsalted butter   heavy cream

† other suitable fish
flounder, sea trout

In this terrine, a duo of sole fillets and a smooth salmon mousseline create a delicate contrast of color and flavor. A simple butter sauce, flavored with citrus juice and ginger, is served with the terrine. This makes a good main-course luncheon dish accompanied by lightly cooked asparagus.

GETTING AHEAD

The terrine can be baked 1 day ahead and kept, covered, in the refrigerator. Before serving, reheat it in a water bath on top of the stove, allowing 10–15 minutes, with the water at a simmer. Make the sauce just before serving.

SHOPPING LIST

1½ lb	fresh salmon fillet
3	egg whites
	salt and pepper
1½ cups	heavy cream
4	sole fillets
	butter for terrine mold
2	slices smoked salmon, total weight about 3 oz
	For the citrus-ginger sauce
3–5	sprigs of parsley
1-inch	piece of fresh ginger root
1	lemon
1	lime
3 tbsp	heavy cream
¾ cup	unsalted butter, chilled

ORDER OF WORK

1. **PREPARE THE SALMON MOUSSELINE**

2. **ASSEMBLE AND BAKE THE TERRINE**

3. **MAKE THE CITRUS-GINGER SAUCE**

1 PREPARE THE SALMON MOUSSELINE

1 Run the blade of the small knife over the salmon fillet to find any bones. Pinch the bones between your thumb and the small knife blade and pull to remove them.

2 If necessary, skin the salmon fillet. Rinse the salmon with cold water and pat dry, then cut into pieces.

ANNE SAYS
"To skin the fillet, set skin-side down and, holding the tail, cut through to the skin at the tail end. Cut the flesh from the skin."

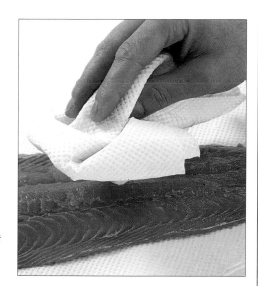

3 Put the salmon pieces in the food processor. Work the fish until smooth, using the pulse button and scraping down the side with the rubber spatula.

! TAKE CARE !
Do not overwork the fish or it will be tough when cooked.

4 Gradually add the egg whites. Using the pulse button work the mixture until smooth, 1–2 minutes, scraping down the side with the rubber spatula. Mix in salt and pepper. Transfer to a bowl.

After adding egg white, mousseline mixture is smooth and quite stiff

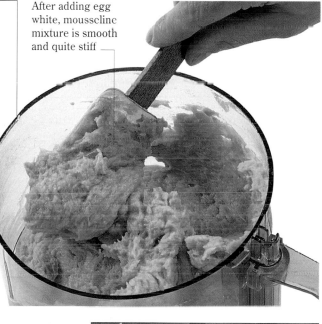

5 Set the bowl in a larger bowl of ice water. Gradually beat in the cream with the wooden spoon, a few tablespoons at a time, stirring well between additions.

ANNE SAYS
"It is best to work in the cream by hand because the mixture could separate if overworked in the food processor."

Pour cream into cool mixture a little at a time

6 Bring a small saucepan of water to a boil. Drop in a little mousseline mixture and simmer until it is firm, 2–3 minutes; it will become lighter in color. Taste it and add salt and pepper to the rest of the mousseline mixture, if needed. Cover the bowl and chill.

2 ASSEMBLE AND BAKE THE TERRINE

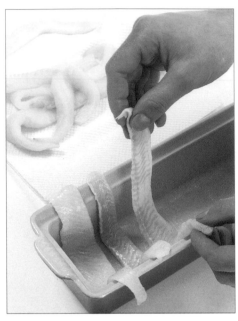

Sole wrapped in smoked salmon gives colorful contrast when terrine is sliced

1 Heat the oven to 350° F. If necessary, skin the sole fillets. Rinse the fillets and pat them dry, then cut each fillet lengthwise in half. Brush the inside of the terrine mold and lid with melted butter.

2 Line the terrine mold with 6 of the sole fillet pieces, arranging them crosswise and skinned side inward.

ANNE SAYS
"Leave gaps between the sole fillet pieces so that the pink salmon mousseline can show through."

3 Wrap each remaining sole fillet lengthwise in a slice of smoked salmon, tucking in the ends neatly.

4 Put one-third of the salmon mousseline into the terrine and spread it evenly with the spatula.

Spread mousseline carefully in mold to avoid air pockets

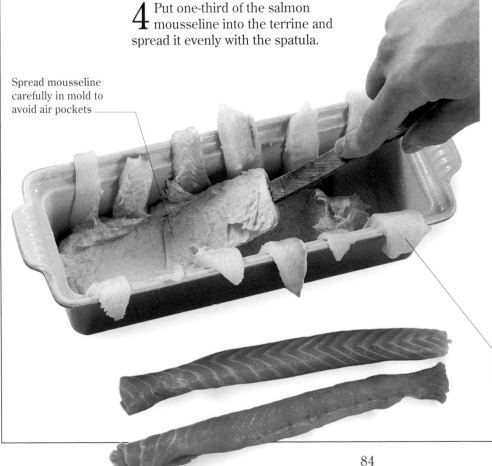

5 Arrange 1 of the smoked salmon and sole fillet cylinders lengthwise on top of the mousseline. Spread another third of the salmon mousseline in the terrine. Top with the second wrapped sole fillet.

Overhanging sole fillets will be wrapped over top when terrine is full

Sole fillets will make attractive bands round cooked mousseline

6 Cover with the remaining mousseline. Using the rubber spatula, smooth the top and press the filling well into the mold.

7 Fold the ends of the sole fillets over the top. Tap the terrine on the work surface to eliminate any air pockets. Put the lid on the terrine mold and set it in the roasting pan.

8 Add hot water to the pan to come just over halfway up the terrine mold. Bring this water bath to a boil on top of the stove, then transfer the terrine in the pan to the heated oven.

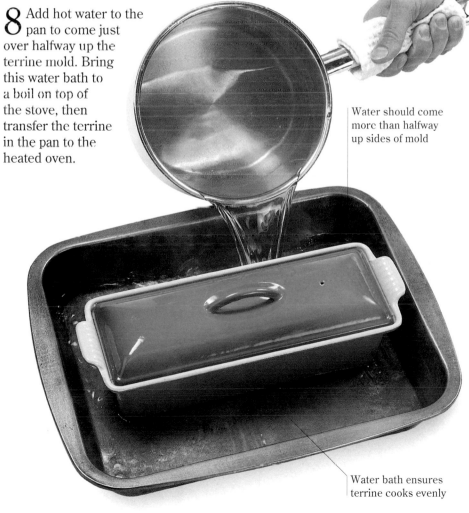

Water should come more than halfway up sides of mold

Water bath ensures terrine cooks evenly

9 Bake until the skewer inserted in the terrine 30 seconds is hot to the touch when withdrawn, 1$\frac{1}{4}$–1$\frac{1}{2}$ hours. Take the terrine from the oven and let stand 5–10 minutes while you make the sauce.

ANNE SAYS
"You can insert the skewer into the terrine through the hole in the lid of the mold."

3 MAKE THE CITRUS-GINGER SAUCE

Gently tear leaves from stems with fingers

Leftover parsley stems are good for flavoring stock and making bouquet garni

1 Strip the parsley leaves from the stems and pile them on the chopping board. With the chef's knife, finely chop the leaves. Peel and finely chop the ginger (see box, below left).

2 Using the vegetable peeler, pare the zest from the lemon. Cut the zest into fine strips. Squeeze the juice from the lemon and reserve it. Squeeze the juice from the lime and reserve.

HOW TO PEEL AND CHOP FRESH GINGER ROOT

It is important to chop ginger root finely, so the flavor spreads evenly throughout the dish.

1 With a small knife, peel the skin from the ginger root. Using a chef's knife, slice the ginger, cutting across the fibrous grain. Place the chef's knife flat on each slice; crush with your hand.

2 Chop the slices of ginger root as finely as possible.

Blanching lemon zest removes any bitterness

3 Bring a small saucepan of water to a boil, add the strips of lemon zest, and simmer 2 minutes. Drain in the strainer and set aside.

4 In a small, heavy-based saucepan, boil the ginger and lemon juice until reduced to 1 tbsp, about 1 minute. Add the cream and boil until reduced to 2 tbsp, about 2 minutes. Cut the chilled butter into pieces.

5 Take the pan from the heat and add the butter, a few pieces at a time, whisking constantly and moving the pan on and off the heat. The butter should thicken the sauce to a creamy consistency without melting to oil.

Lime juice gives sauce extra citrus tang

6 Add the parsley, lemon zest, and lime juice to the sauce. Whisk into the sauce until mixed.

🍴 **TO SERVE**
Turn out the terrine. Cut it into ³/₄-inch slices and serve on pools of sauce on warmed individual plates, alternating sole-banded mousseline slices with unbanded slices.

Asparagus decorated with shreds of lemon zest is complementary accompaniment

7 Holding the lid firmly on the mold, tip it sideways over the saucepan to drain 1–2 tbsp liquid into the sauce. Whisk to mix. Discard the remaining liquid from the terrine. Season the sauce to taste with salt and pepper.

Pink slices of salmon mousseline are studded with sole circled by smoked salmon

VARIATION

INDIVIDUAL FISH TERRINES

Here, ramekins serve as molds for fish terrines. Thin slices of salmon line the molds, with a whiting or sole mousseline filling. The recipe serves 4 people.

1 Butter 4 ramekins (1 cup capacity). Prepare a ³/₄-lb piece of fresh salmon fillet as directed. Holding the salmon steady with your hand and working toward the tail, use a filleting knife to cut large diagonal slices about ¹/₈ inch thick. Cut the slices in half. Line the ramekins with the slices of salmon, allowing excess to hang over the edge.
2 Prepare the mousseline as directed, using 1 lb whiting or sole fillets in place of the salmon. Omit the smoked salmon and additional fish.
3 Spoon the mousseline into the prepared ramekins, smoothing the tops and pressing the filling well into the molds. Fold the salmon edges over the filling, and arrange any remaining salmon slices on top.
4 Cover each with a small round of buttered foil and cook in a water bath as directed, allowing 30–40 minutes.
5 Make the citrus-ginger sauce as directed, but reserve the lemon zest for garnish.
6 Turn out the terrines onto warmed individual plates and spoon the sauce around them. Garnish each terrine with lemon zest; decorate with peeled lime sections and parsley sprigs, if you like.

BOUILLABAISSE

EQUIPMENT

whisk

small knife

chef's knife

vegetable peeler

bowls

large flameproof casserole

strainer

slotted spoon

ladle

wooden spoon

colander

saucepans

paper towels

kitchen string

aluminum foil

chopping board

Purists maintain that a true bouillabaisse cannot be made away from the Mediterranean. However, you can create an excellent version based on local fish – possible white fish include grouper, haddock, orange roughy, perch, pollack, red snapper, and whiting, while among the possible rich fish are eel, mackerel, and striped bass.

*plus 1–2 hours marinating time

INGREDIENTS

mixed white fish

tomatoes

leeks

mixed rich fish

garlic cloves

olive oil

fennel bulb

bouquet garni

onions

Pernod

parsley

orange

tomato paste

celery

saffron threads

ANNE SAYS
"Ask your fish store to trim and scale the fish."

SHOPPING LIST

3 lb	mixed white fish, cleaned, scaled, on bone, with heads
2 lb	mixed rich fish, cleaned, scaled, on bone
2	large pinches of saffron threads
5–6	garlic cloves
1/2 cup	olive oil
2	medium onions
2	medium leeks
2	celery stalks
1	fennel bulb or 1 tsp dried fennel seed
1 lb	tomatoes
1	orange
10–12	sprigs of parsley
1	bouquet garni made with 5–6 parsley stems, 2–3 sprigs of fresh thyme, and 1 bay leaf
1 tbsp	tomato paste
1 tbsp	Pernod or other anise-flavored liqueur
	croûtes (see box, page 89) and Quick Chili Mayonnaise (see box, page 92) for serving (optional)

ORDER OF WORK

1 PREPARE THE FISH, MARINADE, AND STOCK

2 PREPARE THE BROTH

3 FINISH THE BOUILLABAISSE

PREPARE THE FISH, MARINADE, AND STOCK

Saffron gives marinade striking yellow color

1 Rinse the fish inside and out, drain in a colander, and pat dry with paper towels. Keeping the white fish and rich fish separate, cut all the fish across into 2-inch chunks. Reserve the heads and tails for the stock.

ANNE SAYS
"Rinse the fish heads thoroughly to remove any blood which would make the stock bitter."

2 Make the marinade: put 1 large pinch of saffron threads in a small bowl and add 2 tbsp boiling water. Let the saffron soak 10 minutes. Meanwhile, peel and finely chop 2 garlic cloves (see box, page 91). Combine the saffron and its liquid, the finely chopped garlic and 3 tbsp olive oil in a bowl. Stir to mix.

3 Put the white fish chunks in one large non-metallic bowl and the rich fish in another non-metallic bowl. Add half of the marinade to each bowl.

HOW TO MAKE CROUTES

Croûtes – larger versions of the well-known croûtons – are the classic accompaniment to a Provençal bouillabaisse. Here, they are brushed lightly with olive oil and toasted until crisp and browned.

Toast croûtes until dry and lightly browned

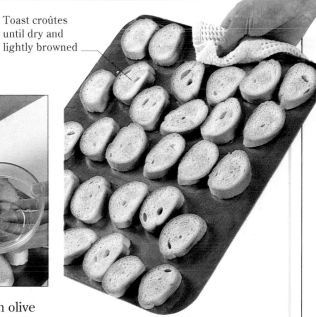

1 Heat the oven to 350° F. Cut 1 loaf of French bread into 3/4-inch slices. Arrange on a baking sheet.

2 Brush the slices lightly with olive oil. Turn them over and brush the other side of each slice.

3 Bake in the heated oven until light brown, 10–12 minutes.

4 Toss the fish to coat thoroughly. Cover and marinate 1–2 hours in the refrigerator.

Stir fish to coat in marinade and ensure flavors are thoroughly absorbed

Keep rich and white fish separate because they will cook at different speeds

5 Meanwhile, make the fish stock: put the heads and tails in a large saucepan, add water barely to cover and bring to a boil. Simmer 20 minutes.

6 Pour the fish stock through the strainer into a bowl and set aside.

2 **PREPARE THE BROTH**

Use tender pale green part of leek tops as well as white portion

1 Peel the onions, leaving a little of the root attached, and cut them in half through the root and stem. Lay each onion half flat on the chopping board and cut across into thin slices.

2 Trim the leeks, discarding the roots and the tough green tops. Slit them lengthwise and wash thoroughly under running water.

3 Cut the leeks crosswise into thin slices using the chef's knife.

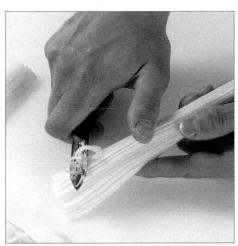

4 With the vegetable peeler, remove the tough strings from each of the celery stalks.

5 Trim the ends from the celery stalks and cut crosswise into thin slices.

Flavor of thinly sliced celery will spread evenly through dish

After strings are removed, celery is easy to slice

6 Trim the base and the feathery green fronds from the fennel bulb.

7 Cut the bulb lengthwise in half, then cut each half into thin slices.

HOW TO PEEL AND CHOP GARLIC

The strength of garlic varies with its age and dryness. Use more when it is very fresh.

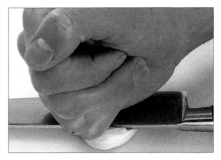

1 To separate the garlic cloves, crush the bulb with the heel of your hand. Alternatively, pull a clove from the bulb with your fingers. To peel the clove, lightly crush it with the flat of the chef's knife to loosen the skin.

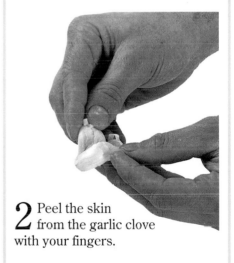

2 Peel the skin from the garlic clove with your fingers.

3 To crush the clove, set the flat side of the knife on top and strike firmly with your fist. Finely chop the garlic with the knife, moving the blade back and forth.

8 Cut the cores from the tomatoes and score an "x" on the base of each with the tip of a knife. Immerse in a pan of boiling water until the skin starts to split, 8–15 seconds depending on their ripeness. Using the slotted spoon, transfer them at once to a bowl of cold water. When cold, peel off the skin. Cut the tomatoes crosswise in half and squeeze out the seeds; coarsely chop each half.

The deeper the color of the tomato, the more flavor it will have

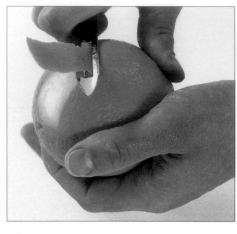

9 Peel a wide strip of zest from the orange with the vegetable peeler. Peel and coarsely chop the remaining garlic cloves.

QUICK CHILI MAYONNAISE

For this quick version of the classic "rouille" or rust-red mayonnaise, bottled mayonnaise and tomato paste are added to chili and garlic.

🍽 SERVES 8–10

🥣 WORK TIME 10 MINUTES

SHOPPING LIST

1	small fresh hot red chili pepper
4	garlic cloves, or to taste
	salt and pepper
¾ cup	bottled mayonnaise
1 tsp	tomato paste
	cayenne (optional)

1 Cut the chili pepper lengthwise in half; discard the core. Scrape out the seeds and cut away the fleshy white ribs from each half. Lightly crush the garlic cloves with the flat of a knife, then peel off the skin.

! TAKE CARE !
Wear rubber gloves to prepare fresh chilis as their oil can burn your skin.

2 Put the chili halves in a food processor with the garlic, salt, and pepper, and finely chop.

3 Add the bottled mayonnaise and tomato paste; purée until smooth. Taste for seasoning and add cayenne, if you like. Refrigerate until serving.

Tomato paste will give mayonnaise appealing pink tinge

12 Heat the remaining oil in the casserole. Add the onions, leeks, celery, and fennel (or fennel seed). Cook, stirring, 5–7 minutes.

10 Strip the parsley leaves from the stems and pile them on the chopping board.

11 With the chef's knife, coarsely chop the parsley leaves. Soak the remaining pinch of saffron threads in 3–4 tbsp boiling water, 10 minutes.

13 Add the tomatoes, orange zest, garlic, and chopped parsley to the casserole.

14 Tie the bouquet garni to the handle of the casserole. Pour in the fish stock. Add the saffron with its liquid and season with salt and pepper. Bring to a boil.

Variety of vegetables will make rich combination of flavors

Fresh taste of parsley is essential accent to dish

15 Simmer the broth until it has thickened and the flavor is mellow, 30–40 minutes, stirring occasionally.

3 FINISH THE BOUILLABAISSE

1 Bring the broth back to a boil. Add the rich fish and boil fiercely, 7 minutes. Shake the casserole from time to time to prevent the mixture from sticking; do not stir or the fish will disintegrate.

ANNE SAYS

"It is important to keep the liquid boiling rapidly so that the oil emulsifies with the broth and does not float on the surface."

Rich fish go into bouillabaisse first because they take longer to cook

Fish will absorb flavor of broth while cooking

2 Add the white fish pieces to the casserole. Set the pieces of the most delicate types of fish on top of the bouillabaisse.

4 With the slotted spoon, transfer the fish to a hot serving platter, arranging them so the different kinds are separated. Cover with foil to keep warm.

3 Continue boiling until the fish just flakes easily with a fork, 5–8 minutes. If necessary, add more water during cooking so the fish remains covered.

Transfer fish carefully or it may fall apart

5 Discard the bouquet garni and orange zest from the broth and whisk in the tomato paste and Pernod. Taste the broth for seasoning.

TO SERVE

Ladle the broth into a soup tureen and serve at once, with the fish. Serve croûtes and chili mayonnaise on the side, if you like.

Fish is served separately from broth; guests can help themselves to each

CREOLE BOUILLABAISSE

In this variation of bouillabaisse, oysters and crayfish join a selection of American fish in the pot. Use redfish, pompano, and grouper as part of the white fish selection, and bluefish with the rich fish, to increase the flavor of the American South.

1 Make croûtes (see box, page 89), rubbing top side with 1–2 peeled garlic cloves before toasting.

2 Prepare and marinate the white fish and rich fish as directed in the main recipe. Peel 1 lb crayfish tails or large shrimp. Slice the green parts of 3 scallions with a chef's knife.

3 Make the bouillabaisse broth as directed in the main recipe, omitting the sprigs of parsley and adding 1 tsp cayenne and 1 tsp dried thyme with the orange zest.

4 Cook the fish in the broth as directed, adding the crayfish, the scallions, and a dozen shucked oysters with their liquid at the same time as the white fish pieces.

5 Serve the fish and broth in individual soup plates, with the garlic croûtes. Garnish with oysters in their shells, if you like.

Spicy mayonnaise can be added to each portion to taste

GETTING AHEAD
The bouillabaisse broth can be made up to 8 hours ahead and kept in the refrigerator. The fish should be cooked in the broth just before serving.

SAUTEED TROUT WITH HAZELNUTS

🍽️ SERVES 4   🥣 WORK TIME 20–25 MINUTES   ♨️ COOKING TIME 10–15 MINUTES

EQUIPMENT

metal spatula

small knife

kitchen scissors

chef's knife   oval fish pan †

wooden spoon

paper towels

aluminum foil

baking sheet

chopping board

† large frying pan can also be used

INGREDIENTS

trout †

hazelnuts   butter

parsley

flour

lemons

† other suitable fish
catfish, mackerel, mullet, perch, whitefish

ANNE SAYS
"*Have your fish store clean the fish through the gills rather than the stomach, to keep their shape better. Or you can do this yourself – see the box on page 113.*"

ORDER OF WORK

1 PREPARE THE TROUT

2 PREPARE THE GARNISH

3 COOK THE TROUT; FINISH THE DISH

In this quick recipe, trout are lightly dusted with seasoned flour, then pan-fried in butter and topped with a mixture of sautéed toasted hazelnuts and chopped parsley. The crunchy topping makes a delicious contrast with the soft textured flesh of the trout, and thin slices of lemon add a fresh accent to the dish. The subtle nutty flavor of a rice pilaf, such as the one on page 74, would marry well with the trout and hazelnuts.

GETTING AHEAD
The trout and hazelnuts are best prepared and sautéed just before serving.

SHOPPING LIST

4	trout, weighing about 10 oz each, cleaned and scaled
½ cup	hazelnuts
5–7	sprigs of parsley
2	lemons
3–4 tbsp	flour
	salt and pepper
½ cup	butter

1 PREPARE THE TROUT

Trimming makes fish more attractive to serve whole

Snip off fins with scissors

1 Cut the fins from the trout with the scissors, and trim the tails to a "V." Rinse the fish inside and out, and pat dry with paper towels.

2 PREPARE THE GARNISH

Skins rub off easily from warm hazelnuts

Hazelnuts will add texture to trout

1 Heat the oven to 350° F. Spread the hazelnuts on the baking sheet and toast them in the heated oven until browned, 8–10 minutes. While still hot, rub the hazelnuts in a dish towel to remove the skins, then let cool.

2 Using the chef's knife, chop the toasted hazelnuts coarsely.

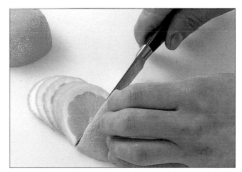

3 Strip the parsley leaves from the stems and pile them on the chopping board. With the chef's knife, chop the leaves coarsely.

4 Trim the ends from 1 of the lemons, then halve the lemon lengthwise and cut it into thin semi-circles, leaving the skin intact.

5 Peel the second lemon (see box, page 98, step 1). Turn the lemon on its side and cut it into thin rounds. Remove any seeds.

HOW TO PEEL AND SECTION A LEMON

Use this method to section a lemon and leave only crescents of flesh.

1 Trim the ends from the lemon. Set the fruit upright and cut away the skin and white pith, following the curve of the fruit.

2 With the lemon in your hand, slide a knife down one side of a section, cutting it from the skin. Cut down the other side; pull out the section. Repeat with remaining sections. Discard any seeds.

ANNE SAYS
"*Section the lemon over a bowl to catch the juice.*"

3 COOK THE TROUT; FINISH THE DISH

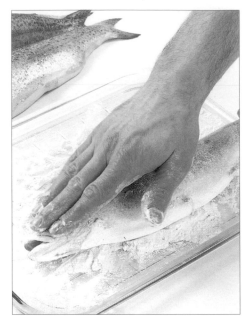

1 Put the flour on a large plate and season with salt and pepper. Coat each trout with the seasoned flour, patting with your hands so each fish is evenly coated.

3 Using the metal spatula, turn the trout over and continue cooking over low heat.

2 Heat half of the butter in the fish pan until it is foaming. Add 2 of the prepared fish to the pan and brown them over medium heat, 2–3 minutes.

4 When ready, the trout will be browned and the flesh will flake easily when tested with a fork, 3–5 minutes. Transfer the fish to a warmed platter and cover with foil to keep warm.

ANNE SAYS
"*When testing if the fish are done, first make a small cut near the head where the flesh is thickest.*"

Turn fish carefully to avoid breaking crisp skin

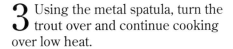

5 Cook the remaining 2 trout, using the rest of the butter. Add the fish to the 2 on the platter, and cover them again with foil.

6 Add the hazelnuts to the fish pan and sauté over medium heat until they are golden brown, stirring constantly, 3–4 minutes.

7 Add three-quarters of the parsley to the pan and stir to mix it with the nuts and browned butter.

Butter should be golden brown so it increases nutty flavor

🍴 **TO SERVE**
Transfer the fish to warmed individual plates, and spoon the hazelnut and parsley mixture over the trout. Decorate with the lemon semi-circles and rounds. Sprinkle with the remaining chopped parsley.

Parsley and hazelnut garnish enhances flavor of freshly caught trout

Rice pilaf is a good contrast to butter sauce on trout

V A R I A T I O N

SAUTEED TROUT WITH CAPERS, LEMON, AND CROUTONS

Small croûtons provide the crunch in this piquant garnish for sautéed trout.

1 Peel and section 3 lemons (see box, page 98). Cut the lemon sections into 3–4 pieces each and gently mix them with 2 tbsp drained capers.

2 Trim the crusts from 2 slices of white bread. Cut the bread into small cubes about the size of the capers.

3 Prepare and cook the trout as directed in the main recipe, using ¼ cup butter. Transfer them to a platter, cover, and keep warm.

4 Wipe out the pan. Add another ⅓ cup butter and fry the bread cubes until golden, 1–2 minutes.

5 Add the capers and lemon pieces, season with salt and pepper, and swirl to combine.

6 Pour the mixture over the fish. Decorate with lemon semi-circles and parsley sprigs and serve at once.

POACHED SALMON WITH WATERCRESS SAUCE

🍽 SERVES 4–6   ⏱ WORK TIME 25–30 MINUTES   ☕ POACHING TIME 15–20 MINUTES

EQUIPMENT

roasting pan†

kitchen scissors

small knife

tweezers

colander

large metal spoon

paper towels

chef's knife

filleting knife

vegetable peeler

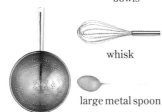
bowls

whisk

citrus juicer

aluminum foil

chopping board

† fish poacher or long deep flameproof dish can also be used

INGREDIENTS

fresh salmon†

lemon

watercress

plain yogurt

bouquet garni

dry white wine

heavy cream

carrot

onion

Tabasco sauce

peppercorns

† other suitable fish
salmon trout, sea bass, sea trout

Poaching in an aromatic liquid called court bouillon is an ideal way to cook a whole salmon or salmon trout, adding flavor, keeping it moist, and making an elegant presentation. Ask the fish store to clean the fish through the stomach.

SHOPPING LIST

4-lb	fresh salmon, cleaned through the stomach
	salt and pepper
	For the court bouillon
1	onion
1	carrot
6	peppercorns
1 cup	dry white wine
1½ quarts	water, more if needed
1	bouquet garni made with 5–6 parsley stems, 2–3 sprigs of fresh thyme, and 1 bay leaf
	For the watercress sauce
1	bunch of watercress
1 cup	heavy cream
1 cup	plain yogurt
1	lemon
	Tabasco sauce

ORDER OF WORK

1 **MAKE THE COURT BOUILLON**

2 **PREPARE AND POACH THE SALMON**

3 **MAKE THE SAUCE**

4 **FINISH THE SALMON**

1 MAKE THE COURT BOUILLON

1 Peel the onion, leaving a little of the root attached, and cut it in half through root and stem. Lay each onion half flat on the chopping board and cut across into medium slices.

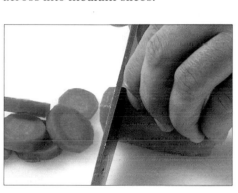

2 Peel the carrot and cut it across into medium slices.

Aromatic ingredients of court bouillon add flavor to poached fish

3 Combine the onion, carrot, peppercorns, white wine, water, and 1 tsp salt in the roasting pan. Add the bouquet garni. Bring to a boil and simmer 20 minutes. Let cool. Meanwhile, prepare the salmon (see page 102).

HOW TO TRIM A FISH

When serving fish whole, trim the fins with kitchen scissors so they do not interfere with serving and cut the tail into a V-shape.

1 Cut the fins from both sides of the fish, then from its belly.

2 Turn the fish over and cut the fins from along the back of the fish.

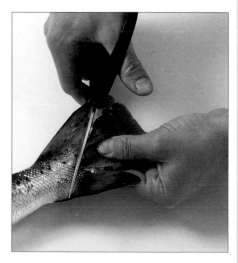

3 Cut a triangle from the tail of the fish to make a neat "V" in the tail.

2 PREPARE AND POACH THE SALMON

1 Scale the salmon (see box, below), then trim the fish (see box, page 101). Using the filleting knife, slit between the ribcage bones and flesh.

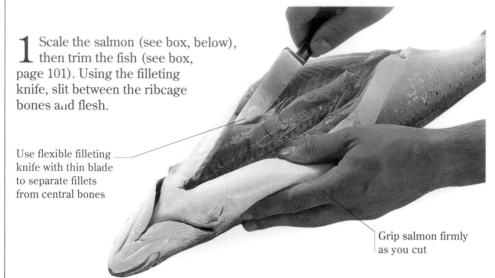

Use flexible filleting knife with thin blade to separate fillets from central bones

Grip salmon firmly as you cut

2 Work toward the backbone, loosening the flesh from the bones on both sides of the ribcage without cutting the skin.

3 Using the scissors, snip the bone at the head to release it. Pull the bone out from the head end.

4 Snip the bone at the tail end to release it. Cut the bone into pieces and reserve. With the tweezers, remove any visible bones from the fish, then run your fingers along the inside of the fish to check that all have been removed.

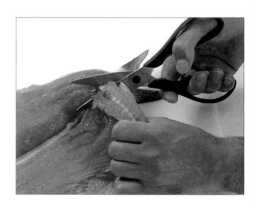

HOW TO SCALE A FISH

Most fish must be scaled before cooking, though often you will find that the fish store has done this. Some fish, such as freshwater trout, have small scales that do not need to be removed. A few fish, such as shark, do not have scales at all.

Fish scales will scatter, so work over draining board or even outdoors

Rinse raw fish before cooking to wash away any remaining impurities

Using the back of a filleting knife, a fish scaler, or a serrated knife held at an angle, scrape off the scales from the whole fish, working from tail to head. Rinse the fish under running water and dry well with paper towels.

5 Rinse the fish inside and out with cold water and pat dry with paper towels.

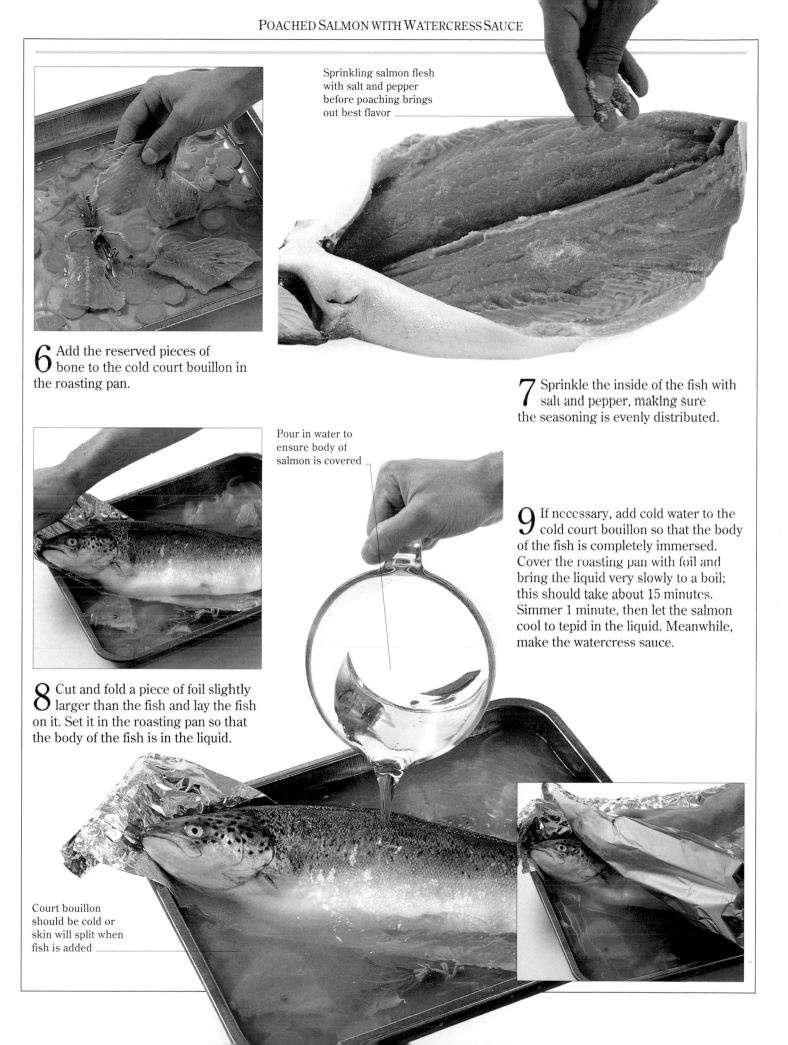

Sprinkling salmon flesh with salt and pepper before poaching brings out best flavor

6 Add the reserved pieces of bone to the cold court bouillon in the roasting pan.

7 Sprinkle the inside of the fish with salt and pepper, making sure the seasoning is evenly distributed.

Pour in water to ensure body of salmon is covered

9 If necessary, add cold water to the cold court bouillon so that the body of the fish is completely immersed. Cover the roasting pan with foil and bring the liquid very slowly to a boil; this should take about 15 minutes. Simmer 1 minute, then let the salmon cool to tepid in the liquid. Meanwhile, make the watercress sauce.

8 Cut and fold a piece of foil slightly larger than the fish and lay the fish on it. Set it in the roasting pan so that the body of the fish is in the liquid.

Court bouillon should be cold or skin will split when fish is added

3 MAKE THE SAUCE

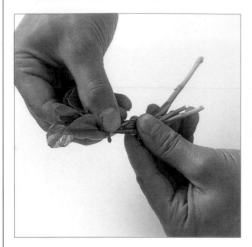  

1 Divide the sprigs of the watercress, then wash them in the colander and dry them thoroughly. Strip the leaves from the stems.

2 Pile the watercress leaves on the chopping board and chop them, using the chef's knife.

3 Whip the cream until soft peaks form. In another bowl, whisk the yogurt until smooth.

4 Add the yogurt to the whipped cream and stir gently to mix them together thoroughly.

Watercress sauce is spiked with lemon juice and Tabasco for tangy accompaniment to poached salmon

5 Add the chopped watercress and a dash of Tabasco sauce. Cut the lemon in half. Squeeze the juice from each half and add to the sauce.

6 Stir the sauce until evenly blended. Add salt and pepper to taste. Cover the bowl and chill until ready to serve.

4 FINISH THE SALMON

1 Holding the ends of the foil, carefully lift the salmon out of the liquid; let drain. Lift the fish off the foil.

Grasp ends of foil firmly to remove salmon from cooking liquid

2 Using the small knife, slit the skin neatly around the head. Repeat around the tail.

3 Peel off the skin from the body, pulling it gently with the help of the small knife. Leave the head and tail intact. Scrape along the back ridge of the fish to remove the line of bones.

4 Using the small knife, gently scrape off any dark flesh from the length of the salmon.

¶◎¶ TO SERVE

Carefully transfer the fish to a large, oval platter and decorate with fresh dill sprigs, salad leaves, tomato wedges, and vegetables, if you like. Serve the watercress sauce separately. Slice the salmon, discarding the head and tail.

Poached salmon is best served at room temperature

— GETTING AHEAD —

The salmon can be poached up to 24 hours ahead and kept, tightly covered, in the refrigerator. Remove the salmon from the refrigerator 20 minutes before serving to allow it to reach room temperature. Peel off the skin just before serving. The watercress sauce can be made up to 4 hours ahead.

Watercress sauce is cool and fresh-tasting

PAN-FRIED MACKEREL COATED IN ROLLED OATS

🍽 SERVES 6　🥄 WORK TIME 15–20 MINUTES　🍲 FRYING TIME 8–12 MINUTES

EQUIPMENT

saucepans

tweezers

large frying pan

strainer

whisk

tongs

paper towels

waxed paper

filleting knife

baking sheet

chopping board

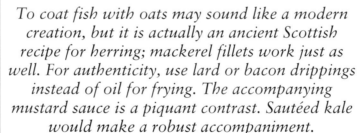

To coat fish with oats may sound like a modern creation, but it is actually an ancient Scottish recipe for herring; mackerel fillets work just as well. For authenticity, use lard or bacon drippings instead of oil for frying. The accompanying mustard sauce is a piquant contrast. Sautéed kale would make a robust accompaniment.

GETTING AHEAD
The fish can be coated up to 2 hours ahead and kept refrigerated. Fry just before serving. The mustard sauce can be made up to 1 hour ahead and kept warm in a water bath.

SHOPPING LIST

3	cleaned mackerel, weighing about ¾–1 lb each
⅓ cup	vegetable oil, more if needed
	salt and pepper
	slices of lemon and parsley sprigs for decoration
	For coating the fish
2	eggs
¼ cup	flour
2 cups	rolled oats
	For the mustard sauce
¼ cup	butter
2 tbsp	flour
1¼ cups	boiling water
	juice of ½ lemon
1 tbsp	Dijon-style mustard, more to taste

INGREDIENTS

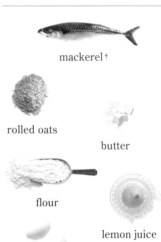

mackerel †

rolled oats

butter

flour

lemon juice

eggs

Dijon-style
mustard

vegetable oil

† other suitable fish

whole cleaned and scaled herring, fillets of flounder or whitefish

ANNE SAYS
"If you prefer to buy your fish already prepared, you can use 6 skinned mackerel fillets, weighing 6 oz each."

ORDER OF WORK

1 PREPARE AND COAT THE MACKEREL

2 MAKE THE MUSTARD SAUCE

3 FRY THE MACKEREL

HOW TO FILLET A ROUND FISH

Round fish, such as salmon, cod, and mackerel, have two fillets that can be cut from either side of the backbone. A well-sharpened filleting knife works best for cutting smooth, even fillets.

1 Starting just behind the head, cut across the fish down to the backbone using a filleting knife.

Hold fish securely with other hand

2 Set the fish on the work surface so that the tail is toward you. Slit the skin along the back from head to tail, holding the knife horizontally.

3 Slide the knife along the upper side of the backbone, carefully detaching the flesh to the mid-point of the fillet.

ANNE SAYS
"A constant cutting motion helps the fillet remain intact."

4 Continue cutting over the rib cage of the fish to free the flesh from the bones and remove the fillet completely.

5 To remove the second fillet, run the knife under the backbone, from head to tail. Sever the fillet from the bone at the tail. Lift off the bone and sever the fillet at the head.

Slide knife as close as possible to backbone to remove flesh neatly

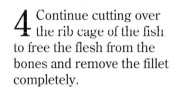

6 Rinse the fillets in cold water and dry on paper towels. If the fish bones are to be used to make stock, rinse them well and reserve them.

HOW TO REMOVE SKIN FROM A FISH FILLET

In many recipes, dark or tough skin is removed from fish fillets before they are cooked.

1 Lay the fillet skin-side down on the work surface with the tail end toward you. Holding the tail end firmly with your fingertips, make a small cut through the flesh just to the skin.

2 Angle the knife so that the cutting edge is against the skin and the blade almost parallel to it. Cut the fish flesh away from the skin, working away from you and using a slight sawing motion, still holding the skin firmly with your other hand.

1 PREPARE AND COAT THE MACKEREL

1 Fillet the mackerel (see box, page 107), then skin the fillets (see box, left). Remove any remaining small bones with the tweezers.

Only tender fish flesh remains after fillets have been skinned

Tweezers are precision tool for taking out small bones

2 Rinse the mackerel fillets again with cold water, put on paper towels, and pat dry.

ANNE SAYS
"Once they have been skinned, the mackerel fillets are quite fragile, so handle them gently."

3 Put the eggs into a shallow dish and beat them with ½ tsp salt just until mixed. Sift the flour onto a sheet of waxed paper.

4 With your fingers, combine the rolled oats, salt, and pepper on a second sheet of waxed paper.

5 Turn each of the mackerel fillets in the flour, so that they are evenly coated, then put them on a plate.

Lift edges of paper to roll and toss fish in oats

6 Dip 1 fillet in the beaten egg to coat it, using 2 forks. Transfer to the oat mixture and coat, tossing with the paper to cover. Dip and coat each remaining fillet.

Oat coating sticks to beaten egg

MAKE THE MUSTARD SAUCE

1 Over low heat, slowly melt one-third of the butter in a medium saucepan.

2 Add the flour to the melted butter in the saucepan and whisk to form a smooth paste. Cook until foaming, about 1 minute.

3 Take from the heat and whisk in the boiling water. The sauce will thicken at once.

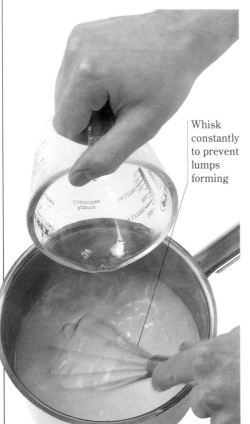

Whisk constantly to prevent lumps forming

4 Return the saucepan to the heat and cook the sauce, whisking constantly, 1 minute. Remove the saucepan from the heat again; add the remaining butter to the sauce and whisk together thoroughly.

5 Add the lemon juice and mustard; whisk to mix. Season to taste with salt, pepper, and more mustard, then whisk again until completely smooth. To keep the sauce warm, set the saucepan in a larger pan of hot water.

! TAKE CARE !
Do not boil or overcook a sauce containing Dijon-style mustard or it will be bitter.

3 FRY THE MACKEREL

1 Heat the oven to very low to keep the fish warm. Line the baking sheet with paper towels. Heat the oil in the frying pan. Add 3 fillets; cook until crisp and golden on the underside, 2–3 minutes.

Fish is cooked in batches so coating does not get soggy

2 Turn the mackerel fillets with the tongs, being careful not to loosen the oat coating.

Flesh should flake
easily with fork

3 Cook until
golden and the fish
flakes easily when tested with
a fork, 2–3 minutes longer. Transfer
to the lined baking sheet; keep warm in
the oven while you fry the remaining
fillets, adding more oil if necessary.

🍴 **TO SERVE**
Arrange the mackerel fillets on a warmed
platter and decorate with halved, twisted
lemon slices and parsley sprigs.
Serve with the warm mustard
sauce on the side.

Mustard sauce is
perfect partner for
crisp-fried fish

Oat coating is
crunchy contrast to
tender mackerel

VARIATION
ALMOND-COATED PERCH

*Ocean perch has sweet-flavored
flesh that marries perfectly with
almonds. Trout fillets can also
be prepared this way.*

1 Omit the mustard sauce from
the main recipe.
2 Chop 1½ cups slivered
almonds and season with salt
and pepper.
3 Rinse and pat dry 6 skinned
perch fillets (about 6 oz each).
Coat as directed for the
mackerel in the main recipe,
substituting the chopped
almonds for the rolled oats.
4 Pan-fry the fish as directed,
over low heat so the almond
coating does not burn, allowing
3–4 minutes on each side.
5 Cut the perch fillets into pieces
and arrange in a decorative pattern on
warmed individual plates.
6 Serve the fillets with potatoes
sautéed in butter and scattered with a
few chopped chives, if you like.

BROILED TROUT WITH ORANGE AND MUSTARD GLAZE

🍽 SERVES 6   🥄 WORK TIME 15–20 MINUTES   ♨ BROILING TIME 20–30 MINUTES

EQUIPMENT

chef's knife

filleting knife   small knife

kitchen scissors

metal spatula

paper towels

tongs

pastry brush

whisk

small bowl

chopping board

ANNE SAYS
"Kitchen scissors for preparing fish should have straight blades and must be strong enough to cut through fish skin and fins."

INGREDIENTS

trout †

honey   Dijon-style mustard

fresh tarragon

vegetable oil

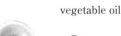
orange juice   tomatoes

mushrooms   Spanish onions

† other suitable fish
perch, pompano, sea bream, whitefish

Broiled whole fish is a dream, quick to prepare and easy to present. Small fish are best because their bones keep them moist and their skin protects them from the intense heat. You can also barbecue the fish, but choose the fuel carefully; strongly flavored woods such as mesquite and hickory can overpower white-fleshed fish.

GETTING AHEAD

The glaze can be made up to 1 week ahead and kept refrigerated. The fish and vegetables can be prepared up to 2 hours ahead, but broil them just before serving.

SHOPPING LIST

6	trout, each weighing ³/₄ lb
6–8	sprigs of fresh tarragon
3	large sweet Spanish onions
3	ripe medium tomatoes
¹/₂ lb	mushrooms
3–4 tbsp	vegetable oil for broiler rack
	For the orange and mustard glaze
¹/₄ cup	Dijon-style mustard
2 tsp	honey
³/₄ cup	orange juice, from 2 oranges
¹/₄ cup	vegetable oil
	salt and pepper

ORDER OF WORK

1 PREPARE THE FISH

2 PREPARE THE VEGETABLES; MAKE THE GLAZE

3 BROIL THE VEGETABLES AND FISH

1 PREPARE THE FISH

2 Strip the tarragon leaves from the stems, then tuck a leaf of tarragon in each slash. Set the fish aside in a cool place.

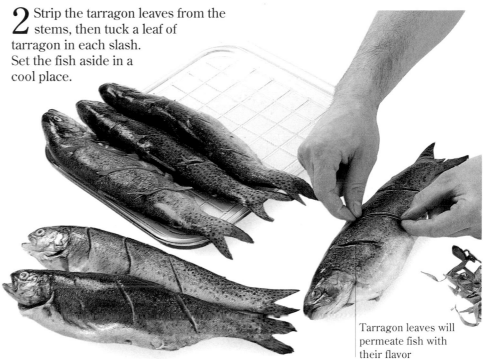

1 Clean the fish through the gills (see box, below). With the scissors, cut the fins from the fish and trim the tails to a "V." Rinse the fish inside and out and pat dry with paper towels. With the filleting knife, slash each fish diagonally 3–4 times on both sides. The slashes should be about ³/8-inch deep to allow heat to penetrate.

Tarragon leaves will permeate fish with their flavor

HOW TO CLEAN A WHOLE FISH THROUGH THE GILLS

Fish to be served whole are cleaned through the gills in order to maintain their shape. If your fish is cleaned by the fish store, make sure you specify "through the gills." If the stomach is cut open, it will curl unattractively during cooking.

Cold running water cleans stomach cavity thoroughly

1 Hook your fingers through the gills and pull them out.

2 Reach through the gill opening and pull out the stomach contents.

! TAKE CARE !
The gills can be quite sharp so be careful when putting in your fingers.

4 Run cold water into the gill opening and out through the ventral opening to clean the cavity thoroughly.

3 With scissors, make a small slit at the ventral or stomach opening and pull out any remaining contents.

2 PREPARE THE VEGETABLES; MAKE THE GLAZE

1 Peel the onions and cut them crosswise into ¹/₂-inch slices, discarding the root and top.

2 Cut the cores from the tomatoes, then cut each one crosswise in half. Wipe the mushroom caps with damp paper towels and trim the stems even with the caps.

3 Make the glaze: whisk the mustard and honey together in the bowl, then whisk in the orange juice. Gradually add the oil, whisking constantly. Season with salt and pepper.

3 BROIL THE VEGETABLES AND FISH

1 Heat the broiler. Brush the rack generously with oil. Arrange the onion slices and mushrooms on the rack. Brush them with a little of the glaze and sprinkle with salt and pepper.

Brush glaze to edge of each onion slice

Honey-mustard glaze moistens vegetables and broils to golden finish

2 Broil the onions and mushrooms about 3 inches from the heat, brushing with a little more glaze and turning occasionally with the tongs, allowing about 3 minutes for the mushrooms and 5–7 minutes for the onions; they should be slightly charred. Remove and keep warm.

3 Cook the tomatoes skin-side toward the heat until warmed through and the skin is slightly charred, 5–7 minutes; do not turn them. Remove and keep warm.

4 Place the fish on the rack (in 2 batches if necessary). Brush with glaze; sprinkle with salt and pepper. Broil until browned, 4–7 minutes.

Flake flesh gently with fork to test

5 Carefully turn the fish using the metal spatula and brush each with more glaze. Continue broiling until the flesh just flakes easily when tested with a fork, 4–7 minutes more.

ANNE SAYS
"*Cooking time depends on the thickness of the fish, measured at the thickest point. For every inch of thickness, allow 10 minutes cooking time.*"

Crispy trout skin is coated with delicious honey-mustard glaze

▮◉▯ TO SERVE
Place the fish on warmed individual plates. Accompany with the vegetables and a decoration of lamb's lettuce, if you like. Spoon any remaining glaze over the fish.

BROILED COD STEAKS WITH MAITRE D'HOTEL BUTTER

These broiled cod steaks are topped with pats of butter flavored with parsley, shallot, and lemon.

1 Omit the glaze. Peel 1 shallot and set it flat-side down on a chopping board. Slice horizontally toward the root, leaving the slices attached at the root. Slice vertically, then cut across the shallot to make fine dice.

2 Strip the leaves from 8–10 parsley stems and pile them on the chopping board. Finely chop the leaves.

3 Cream ⅓ cup butter. Mix in the shallot, parsley, the juice of ½ lemon, salt, and pepper. Spoon the butter onto a piece of waxed paper or plastic wrap and shape into a roll, twisting the ends to seal. Refrigerate until firm.

4 Rinse and pat dry 6 cod steaks (total weight 2 ½ lb). Brush them with 3–4 tbsp olive oil, sprinkle with salt and pepper, and broil 3–5 minutes on each side. Brush with more olive oil and sprinkle with more salt and pepper after turning the steaks.

5 Set a slice of the maître d'hôtel butter on top of each cod steak and serve, accompanied by grated carrot with a scattering of dill, if you like.

SOLE BONNE FEMME

🍴 SERVES 4 🥄 WORK TIME 30–35 MINUTES 🍲 COOKING TIME 25–30 MINUTES

EQUIPMENT

bowls

frying pan

chef's knife

filleting knife

pastry brush

baking dish

kitchen scissors

saucepans

wooden spoon

slotted spatula

whisk

large metal spoon

ladle

chopping board

aluminum foil

strainer

paper towels

In this most delicious of fish dishes, fillets of sole are poached in fish stock, which forms the basis for a creamy velouté sauce. The bones from the filleted sole can be used for the fish stock.

GETTING AHEAD
The fish can be filleted and the fish stock prepared up to 4 hours in advance. Keep in the refrigerator until needed, making sure the fish is covered.

SHOPPING LIST

2	whole sole, weighing 2 lb each, cleaned and scaled	
2	shallots	
½ lb	mushrooms	
1 tbsp	butter, more for baking dish and foil	
	salt and pepper	
3–4 tbsp	water	
	For the fish stock	
1	onion	
2 cups	cold water, more if needed	
3–5	sprigs of parsley	
1 tsp	peppercorns	
1 cup	white wine or juice of 1 lemon	
	For the sauce	
2 tbsp	butter	
2 tbsp	flour	
3 tbsp	heavy cream	
3	egg yolks	
	juice of ½ lemon, or to taste	

INGREDIENTS

sole†

egg yolks

heavy cream

white wine

butter

mushrooms

flour

shallots

parsley

onion

peppercorns

lemon juice

---
† other suitable fish
flounder, pompano, whitefish

ORDER OF WORK

1 PREPARE THE SOLE

2 MAKE THE FISH STOCK

3 PREPARE THE MUSHROOMS; POACH THE SOLE

4 MAKE THE SAUCE AND FINISH THE DISH

1 PREPARE THE SOLE

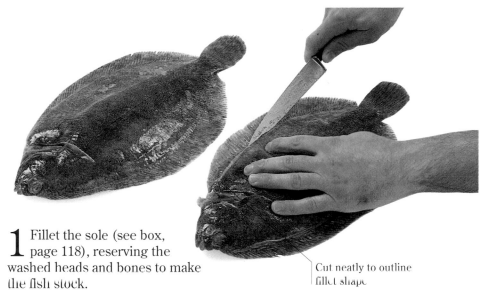

1 Fillet the sole (see box, page 118), reserving the washed heads and bones to make the fish stock.

Cut neatly to outline fillet shape

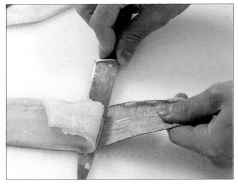

2 Set each fillet skin-side down and hold the tail firmly. Cut through to the skin at the tail end, then angle the knife, and cut the flesh from the skin, using a sawing motion. Rinse the fillets and pat dry with paper towels.

MAKE THE FISH STOCK

1 Cut the washed fish heads and bones into 4–5 pieces with the chef's knife.

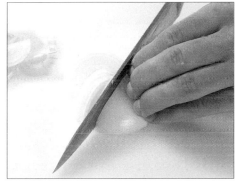

2 Peel the onion, leaving a little of the root attached, and cut it in half through root and stem. Cut each half vertically into thin slices.

Stock is clear and light if bones are washed well

3 Put the fish heads and bones in a medium saucepan. Add the onion, water, parsley, and peppercorns. Pour in the wine.

4 Bring to a boil and simmer about 20 minutes, skimming occasionally with the large spoon.

! TAKE CARE !
Do not simmer the stock too long or it will be bitter.

5 Pour the fish stock through the strainer into a second saucepan, to remove all flavoring ingredients.

ANNE SAYS
"Do not season the stock because the flavors will intensify when it is reduced."

HOW TO FILLET A FLATFISH

Flatfish, such as sole and flounder, are usually cut into four fillets, two on either side of the central bones. The filleting technique is quite similar to that used for round fish.

1 With the point of a filleting knife, cut around the edge of the fish to outline the shape of the fillets. With the point of the knife, cut the fish to the bone in a semicircle behind the head.

Hold fish steady to cut accurately with other hand

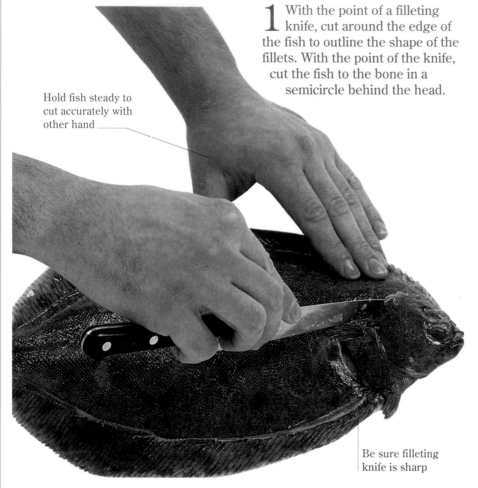

Be sure filleting knife is sharp

2 Cut through to the bone, along the spine at the center of the fish, in a straight line from head to tail.

3 Keeping the knife almost flat, slip the blade between the flesh and the rib bones and cut away the fillet, using a stroking motion.

4 Continue cutting until the fillet and flesh lying along the fins are detached with the skin in one piece. Turn the fish around and slip the knife under the flesh of the second fillet. Detach the fillet from the bones as for the first fillet.

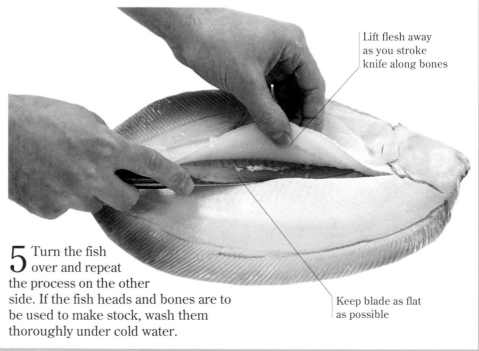

Lift flesh away as you stroke knife along bones

Keep blade as flat as possible

5 Turn the fish over and repeat the process on the other side. If the fish heads and bones are to be used to make stock, wash them thoroughly under cold water.

3 PREPARE THE MUSHROOMS; POACH THE SOLE

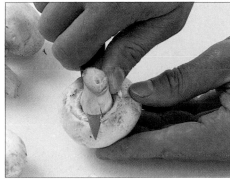

1 Heat the oven to 350° F. Peel the shallots and separate into sections, if necessary. Slice horizontally toward the root, leaving the slices attached. Slice vertically, leaving the root end uncut; cut across to make fine dice.

2 Wipe the mushroom caps with damp paper towels and trim the stems even with the caps. Set the mushrooms stem-side down on the chopping board and slice them.

3 Melt the butter in the frying pan; add the mushrooms with salt, pepper, and water. Cover with buttered foil and cook until the mushrooms are tender when tested with the small knife, 5 minutes. Set aside.

Fillets should not be completely immersed in stock

4 Butter the baking dish; sprinkle the shallots over the bottom. Fold each sole fillet in half, with the skinned side inward, and arrange on the shallots, tail upward. Season the fish with salt and pepper.

5 Ladle enough fish stock over the fillets to half cover them. Top with a piece of buttered foil.

6 Poach the fish in the heated oven until it just flakes easily when tested with a fork, 15–18 minutes.

7 Using the slotted spatula, transfer each sole fillet to paper towels to drain, reserving the fish cooking liquid. Keep the fillets warm while making the sauce.

4 MAKE THE SAUCE AND FINISH THE DISH

1 Add the fish cooking liquid with the shallots to the remaining stock; boil until it has reduced to 1^1/$_2$ cups.

2 Melt the butter in a separate saucepan. Whisk in the flour. Cook until foaming, 1–2 minutes. Remove the pan from the heat and let cool slightly.

3 Strain the reduced stock into the butter and flour mixture. Return to the heat and bring to a boil, whisking constantly until thickened. Reduce the heat and let simmer 5 minutes.

Mushroom slices add essential flavor and make attractive decoration for final dish

4 Remove the sauce from the heat. Add the mushrooms with their cooking liquid and stir to mix.

5 Mix the cream and egg yolks in a small bowl, using the whisk.

6 Ladle a little of the hot sauce into the cream and egg yolk mixture and whisk to mix.

7 Stir the cream mixture into the remaining sauce in the pan. Return to the heat and cook gently, stirring, until it thickens enough to coat the back of the spoon (your finger will leave a trail across the spoon), 2–3 minutes. Do not boil the sauce or it will curdle. Remove from the heat. Add lemon juice, salt, and pepper to taste.

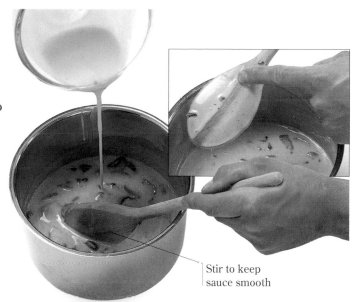

Stir to keep sauce smooth

8 Heat the broiler. Arrange 2 fillets on each of 4 flameproof plates. Ladle the sauce over the fish, so it is completely coated. Broil until lightly browned and glazed, 1–2 minutes.

TO SERVE

Serve the sole at once, garnished with sprigs of fresh herbs, if you like. Boiled rice is an excellent accompaniment.

Boiled rice is perfect with rich sauce and can be shaped neatly in a timbale mold

VARIATION

FILLETS OF SOLE WITH MUSHROOMS AND TOMATOES

Poached sole fillets with a mushroom and tomato-speckled sauce are a colorful variation of Sole Bonne Femme.

1 Cut the cores from 2 tomatoes and score an "x" on the base of each with the tip of a knife. Immerse them in boiling water until the skin starts to split, 8–15 seconds depending on their ripeness. Transfer at once to a bowl of cold water. When cold, peel off the skin. Cut the tomatoes crosswise in half and squeeze out the seeds. Finely chop each half.
2 Prepare the sole, fish stock, and mushrooms as directed.
3 Poach the sole fillets as directed, adding the tomatoes to the baking dish with the shallots.
4 Strip the leaves from 10–12 parsley sprigs and pile them on a chopping board. Finely chop the leaves.
5 Make the sauce, adding the fish cooking liquid to 1/2 cup white wine instead of the remaining fish stock. Pour the reduced liquid into the butter and flour mixture without straining. When the sauce thickens, whisk in 11/2 tbsp tomato paste.
6 Add the chopped parsley with the mushrooms and their liquid.
7 Ladle the sauce over the fish arranged on flameproof plates and broil as directed. Serve with yellow pattypan squashes, if you like.

FISH KNOW-HOW

The wide variety of fish on the market allows the cook an abundant choice. However, different types of fish have different characteristics, and it is helpful to be aware of appropriate substitutes. Because fish is a highly perishable food it is also important to know the best methods for storage and handling. Fish lends itself to many cooking methods and its delicate texture means that microwaving can be an ideal treatment.

CHOOSING FISH

Choosing fish is not as straightforward as buying a cut of meat, because there are no government guidelines to quality. Luckily, a fish in impeccable condition is easy to spot. Look for the following features:

• Fish should smell fresh and clean, without a strong or unpleasant "fishy" odor.

• For whole fish, the scales should be intact and shiny, the eyes clear and full with no cloudiness, and the gills should be bright pink or red, not dull or brown.

• All fish should feel firm and resilient, not soft or spongy, when pressed with a fingertip.

• Fish fillets should not be dry or discolored, nor should they be wet or watery.

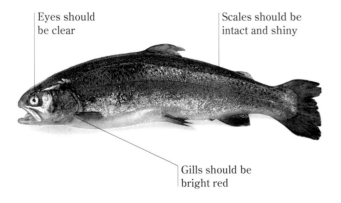

Eyes should be clear

Scales should be intact and shiny

Gills should be bright red

ANNE SAYS
"A fish that has been cut into steaks or fillets deteriorates more rapidly than a whole fish because the exposed flesh is more vulnerable to bacteria. For this reason it is better to buy fish at a store that prepares portions on the spot rather than buying pre-cut fish steaks and fillets. Better still, purchase whole fish and cut fillets yourself, because whole fish will remain fresher longer."

FISH GROUPS

Fish is almost the only remaining food that is caught mainly in the wild rather than being farmed. As a result, supplies are unpredictable, varying enormously in type and quality from season to season and area to area. Therefore when you shop for fish, you may not always find the fish you want. It is important to know which fish can be substituted for others, and suggestions for alternative fish are given in each recipe. Note that a few fish are now farmed – trout, salmon, catfish, and striped bass are outstanding examples – so you are more likely to find them on a consistent basis.

Most important for cooking fish is an understanding of the differences in taste, texture, and bone structure among the various types. A fish with oily, rich flesh is as different from a white-fleshed fish as duck is from chicken. Texture is another important characteristic: the coarse flesh of cod differs from the fine texture of sole and neither could be confused with the firmness of tuna or the delicate pink flesh of salmon.

When you must substitute one fish for another in a recipe, it is important to keep the following groups in mind so that you can choose a fish that is most appropriate in texture and flavor for the given preparation.

COD FAMILY

Cod, haddock, hake, and pollack are all members of the same family and form almost half of the world's commercial fish catch. Usually too large to sell whole, they are most often cut into steaks or fillets. They resemble one another in many respects, with white, firm flesh which produces large flakes. Not only are these fish abundant, but they yield full-flavored, thick flesh that is highly adaptable. Fish in the cod family are excellent broiled, sautéed, steamed, baked, or deep-fried with any number of sauces and accompaniments. You can substitute one for another without hesitation.

FLATFISH

Most types of small flatfish look very alike and can be easily substituted one for another. Indeed in most fish stores, small flatfish are always sold filleted under the generic names of sole, flounder, or whitefish. Flatfish, as the name suggests, are flat, with a lateral bone structure and spine that produce four fillets, unlike the two fillets of all round fish. Many flatfish weigh a mere $^3/_4$–1 lb and are ideal as an individual serving on the bone; they can be pan-fried whole or simply scored and baked in the oven with parsley, a little butter, and some white wine. The flesh of all these fish is delicate and fine-textured, best left to simple preparations such as poaching, baking, and pan-frying. Halibut is the only large flatfish commonly available. It is sold as steaks or fillets and a firm fish like cod is the nearest equivalent.

WHITE FISH

Many popular fish have flesh that is white in color and mild in flavor. Well-loved red snapper and orange roughy and two freshwater fish, catfish and perch, are among the fish from this group that offer succulent flesh with an excellent flavor. Alternatives are grouper and mahi mahi. The size of white fish varies enormously, with some species available whole, while others are sold only cut in fillets and steaks because they are so large. Their firm flesh makes them appropriate for all cooking methods. Mullet has softer flesh, and is best poached, steamed, or sautéed so that it remains moist.

MEATY FISH

Two well-known fish, tuna and swordfish, highlight this category, and are inter-changeable in many recipes. Tuna is a rich fish that must be eaten as fresh as possible, particularly darker types such as bluefin. Albacore, the only white-fleshed tuna, is preferred for canning. Swordfish, also white-fleshed, is always sold in steaks, while depending on the variety, tuna comes as steaks or in big pieces resembling a cut of meat. Broiling and outdoor grilling are favorite methods for cooking both of these meaty fish, with roasting and pan-frying as alternatives.

MONKFISH

This fish has a huge unattractive head, so you will find only the tail meat in the fish store, either whole, in fillets, or in steaks. The flesh is mild, slightly sweet, and chewy, and does not overcook easily. Another advantage for the cook is its straight spinal cord: the fact that it has no lateral small bones makes it easy to fillet. Baking and sautéing are good uses for monkfish, and its firm flesh is ideal in fish stews. There is no direct substitute although there are possible alternatives in individual recipes.

SALMON AND TROUT

Salmon and trout look alike and are closely related. Salmon, with its deep pink flesh and delectable flavor, is divided into two groups, Pacific and Atlantic. It is sold whole weighing from 5–15 lb, and in fillets and steaks. The most familiar variety of trout is rainbow, which is often farmed and sold whole as a single portion (weighing $3/4$–l lb). Salmon trout has the pink flesh of salmon with the firm texture of trout. The rich flesh of all these fish is ideal for baking, poaching, and sautéing, not to mention outdoor grilling.

RICH FISH

Fish in this group, such as mackerel, herring, sardines, sea bass, and striped bass, tend to have a characteristic flavor. Their flesh is soft and flaky and holds its shape well. Most weigh under 5 lb, but some can be small enough to need several per portion. Absolute freshness is a prerequisite for all rich fish because their high oil content oxidizes and turns rancid rapidly. Despite their richness, they are good pan-fried, since this seals in flavor, and they are also good broiled, baked, or grilled over an open fire. Acid flavorings, such as lemon, vinegar, and sour cream, help to balance their richness, as witness the international popularity of pickled herring.

STORING FISH

Store fresh fish for as short a time as possible. To some extent, shelf-life depends on the type and quality of the fish. A reliable retailer is important, so you can be sure of the age of the fish before deciding how long it can be stored at home. Temperature is the key to maintaining quality. Spoilage occurs twice as fast at 40° F (the usual temperature of a home refrigerator) than at 32° F, which is the ideal storage temperature for fish, so always keep fish in the coldest part of the refrigerator.

Freshly caught whole fish keep longer if they have been gutted because this eliminates the enzymes in the stomach that accelerate decay. Fish fillets and pieces should be used within 24 hours. In general, rich fish such as mackerel spoil more rapidly than white fish such as cod and sole. Fish stored in a home refrigerator should be wrapped tightly in plastic and covered in ice. Note that cut fish should not come into direct contact with ice because this will discolor the flesh and draw out its juices. As the ice melts take care to drain the water to keep the fish from deteriorating.

FREEZING & THAWING FISH

Freezing fish at home must be done very carefully. Home freezers chill food more slowly than commercial machines, allowing the formation of ice crystals, which penetrate the cell walls of the fish damaging the flavor and texture. If you must freeze fish, make sure the freezer is set at its lowest temperature. Clean whole fish, and wash it thoroughly, handling it as gently as possible, then wrap it in freezer wrap. Steaks and fillets can also be frozen, carefully wrapped. Rich fish, such as salmon, and firm-fleshed white fish, such as cod, freeze better than delicate ones such as flounder. If carefully frozen, fish can keep up to 3 months in the freezer.

It is best to thaw frozen fish slowly in the refrigerator before cooking, to maintain texture and minimize moisture loss. You should allow a few hours per pound of fish. Some cooks like to cook small frozen fish fillets without thawing them; cooking times must be increased accordingly.

FISH STOCK

Fish stock is an indispensable ingredient in many sauces, soups, and chowders. Bones, heads, and tails of lean white fish, especially flatfish, such as sole, are recommended for stock. Avoid rich fish such as mackerel that can make stock oily. Fish stock keeps well up to 2 days if it is kept covered in the refrigerator, or it can be frozen.

🍽️ MAKES ABOUT 1 QUART

🥣 WORK TIME 10–15 MINUTES

🍲 COOKING TIME 20 MINUTES

SHOPPING LIST

$1^1/_2$ lb	fish bones and heads
1	onion
1 cup	white wine or juice of $^1/_2$ lemon
1 quart	water
3–5	sprigs of parsley
1 tsp	peppercorns

1 Thoroughly wash the fish bones and heads. Cut the bones into 4–5 pieces with a chef's knife. Peel the onion, leaving a little of the root attached, and cut it in half through the root and stem. Lay each onion half on a chopping board and cut it vertically into thin slices.

2 Put the fish bones and heads in a medium saucepan with the onion slices, wine or lemon juice, water, parsley sprigs, and peppercorns. Bring to a boil and simmer 20 minutes. Skim the stock occasionally with a large metal spoon.

! TAKE CARE !
Do not simmer fish stock too long or it will be bitter.

3 Strain the stock into a bowl. Let cool, then cover and keep in the refrigerator.

ANNE SAYS
"I never season stock with salt and ground pepper at the time of making, because it might be reduced later in individual recipes and the flavors will intensify."

SERVING SIZES

Fish range enormously in size, but when you are buying fresh fish, a few simple guidelines will help you decide how much to buy. For large or individual fish, such as salmon or trout, and small flatfish, such as sole, that are to be served whole on the bone with the head intact, allow $^3/_4$–1 lb per person. If the fish is to be served on the bone but with the head removed, count on $^1/_2$–$^3/_4$ lb per person. Other factors that influence the size of portions are the leanness of the fish, whether the fish is stuffed, cooked with other ingredients or served with a rich sauce,

the role the dish plays within the meal, and the size of appetites. For fish fillets and fish steaks that have little or no bone, 6–8 oz per person is the usual portion.

FISH AND YOUR HEALTH

Low in fat and high in protein, fish has always been a star as far as healthy cooking is concerned. Fish lends itself well to low-calorie methods of cooking, including poaching, steaming, grilling, and broiling. *Steamed Braided Fish with Warm Vinaigrette* is a recipe that is low in fat; you can eliminate the added fat altogether by omitting the warm vinaigrette and serving the fish with a simple squeeze of lemon juice. *Broiled Tuna Steaks with Salsa* has a minimum of added fat, as does *Oriental Halibut in a Paper Case* and both incorporate a healthy fresh vegetable accompaniment. *Poached Salmon with Watercress Sauce* is yet another healthy choice, served with a yogurt sauce.

The richness of other recipes can be reduced by leaving out accompaniments. Omit the sauces from *Roast Monkfish with Garlic and Chili Sauces* and enjoy the plainly roasted, herb-coated fish; likewise serve *Bouillabaisse* plain, without the chili sauce. Cook the *Tuna and Bacon Kebabs* without the bacon; the broiled marinated tuna will be delicious on its own, and lighter without the meat. And don't forget, when frying and sautéing, butter can be replaced with olive or polyunsaturated margarine.

MICROWAVE

Cooking fish is one of the great strengths of the microwave. The speed of the microwave ensures that the naturally delicate flesh of fish stays moist, but also cooks evenly. The texture and flavor of fish are also better preserved than with most conventional cooking methods. For example, you will find that *Steamed Braided Fish with Warm Vinaigrette* can be cooked more quickly in a microwave than in a steamer, with the same if not better results. *Poached Salmon with Watercress Sauce* cooks in a microwave perfectly – the fish can be curled into a circle for cooking if necessary. *Turbans of Sole with Wild Mushroom Mousse* is yet another recipe that is ideal for cooking in the microwave oven, though don't try to reheat the butter sauce in the microwave once the butter has been added, and make sure the turbans are evenly spaced, and not touching, so that each cooks in the same time. Soups and stews, including *Spicy Fish Stew* and *New England Cod and Mussel Chowder*, can be made very successfully and more rapidly in the microwave.

Many other dishes in this book can be adapted to a combination of microwave and conventional cooking. Sauté the monkfish pieces for *Monkfish Américaine* on top of the stove, then make the Américaine sauce in the microwave. Boil the lasagne noodles for *Seafood Lasagne* conventionally, then cook the assembled dish in the microwave; just before serving, it may need cooking briefly under a hot broiler to brown the top. *English Fish Pie* can be partially prepared in the microwave, including preparing the sauce and making the mashed potato topping, but do not hard-boil the eggs in the microwave because steam will build up in the shells making them burst. The assembled pie is best baked in the conventional oven.

Here are a few tips to remember when microwaving fish:

• Place thicker fish parts toward the edge of the dish and tuck under thin ends.

• Shield delicate or thin parts of fillets and whole fish with small pieces of very smooth aluminum foil.

• Whole fish, particularly large ones, should be slightly undercooked, then left to stand, covered, because they will continue cooking in their own heat.

• Rotate whole fish or fish fillets during microwaving to ensure even cooking.

• Turn over thick pieces of fish halfway through cooking or the juices that collect in the dish will distribute extra heat to only one side of the fish, cooking it unevenly.

• Excess moisture from microwaved fish can be absorbed by lining the dish with paper towels.

• Do not reheat fish in the microwave; fish cooks so quickly that the flesh will dry out too much.

HOW-TO BOXES

*There are pictures of all preparation steps for each **Fish Classics** recipe. Some basic techniques are general to a number of recipes; they are shown in extra detail in these special "how-to" boxes.*

INDEX

ACKNOWLEDGMENTS

Photographers David Murray
Jules Selmes
Assisted by Ian Boddy

Chef Eric Treuille
Cookery Consultant Linda Collister
Assisted by Joanna Pitchfork

US Editor Jeanette Mall

Typesetting Linda Parker
Rowena Feeny
Robert Moore
Deborah Rhodes

Text film by Disc to Print (UK) Limited

Production Consultant Lorraine Baird

*Anne Willan would like to thank her
chief editor Kate Krader, associate
editor Stacy Toporoff, and consultant
editor Cynthia Nims for their vital
help with writing this book and
researching and testing the recipes,
aided by Jacqueline Bobrow and
La Varenne's chefs and trainees.*